CONTENTS

ARCHITECTURE

Architectural highlights on route 1 range from the colonial to the contemporary. Route 15 explores the ancient walled villages of the New Territories. For European style, head to Macau (routes 17 and 18).

RECOMMENDED ROUTES FOR…

ART BUFFS

Artistic highlights include the galleries around Hollywood Road (route 4), Wan Chai's Arts Centre (route 6), the Hong Kong Museum of Art and the Hong Kong Heritage Discovery Centre (route 10).

BEACHES

In need of a break from the city backdrop? Some of the area's most accessible beaches are on the Southside (route 9), and less crowded ones are dotted around Lamma (route 14).

DINING OUT

There is great regional Chinese cuisine available everywhere and good international options in Lan Kwai Fong and SoHo (route 5), Wan Chai (route 7), Southside (route 9) and Tsim Sha Tsui (route 10).

FAMILY

Animal-lovers should visit the pandas, dolphins and other creatures at Ocean Park (route 9). Science fans may prefer the Space Museum (route 10). For a treat with some familiar faces, head out to HK Disneyland (route 13).

NIGHT OWLS

Bars and restaurants open late across the city, but good starting points for night-time action include Lan Kwai Fong and SoHo (route 5), Wan Chai (route 7) and Tsim Sha Tsui (route 10).

SHOPPING

There are traditional stores in Sheung Wan (route 2), malls in Shenzhen (route 16), flea markets in Cat Street (route 4), electronics and tailors along Nathan Road (route 10) and markets (route 11) in Kowloon.

TEMPLES AND MONASTERIES

Of the many fine temples in Hong Kong, among the best are the Man Mo (route 4) and Pak Tai Temple (route 6). The giant bronze Buddha at Po Lin Monastery draws crowds (route 12).

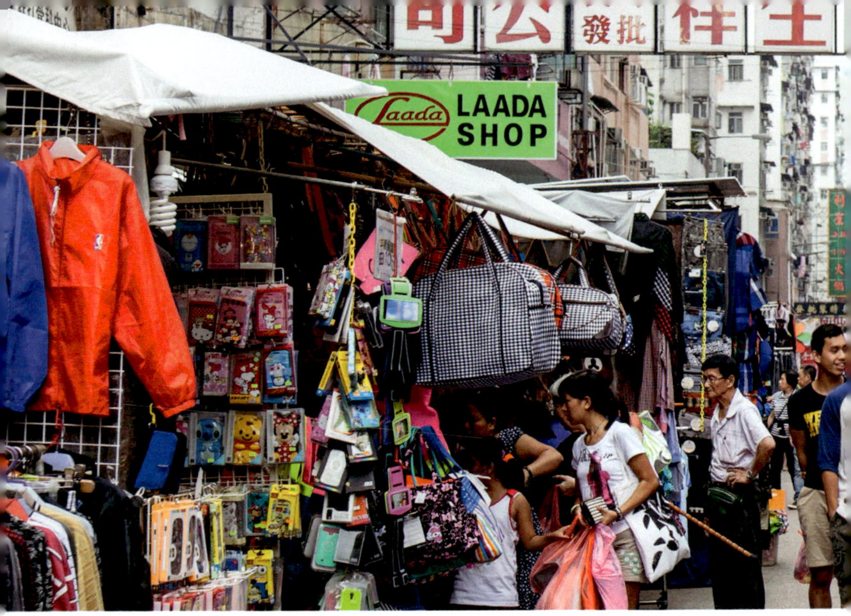
發批
Laada
LAADA
SHOP

Stanley Market Road
赤柱市場道 12-6

$22
$22

發財
福

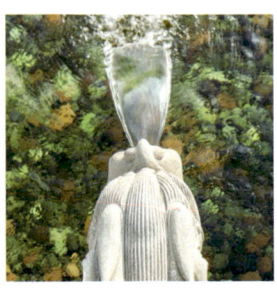

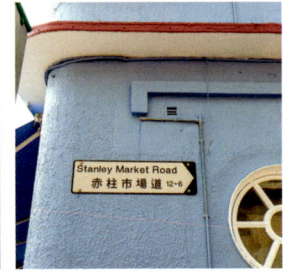

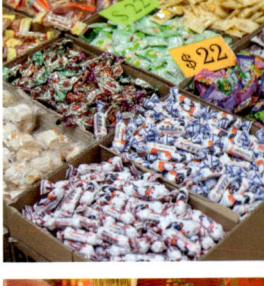

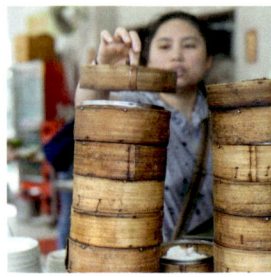

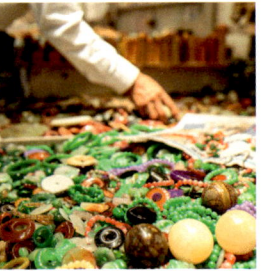

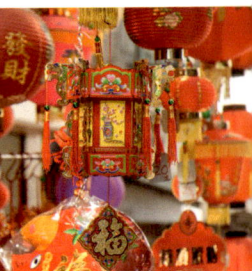

INTRODUCTION

An introduction to Hong Kong's geography, customs and culture, plus illuminating background information on cuisine, history and what to do when you're there.

In Lin Heung Teahouse

EXPLORE HONG KONG

Hong Kong is one of the most vibrant cities in the world, and it is also one of the most straightforward and safe to explore. Signposts are in English as well as Chinese, while inexpensive public transport and taxis make it easy to get around.

Covering 1,104 sq km (426 sq miles) Hong Kong, a Special Administrative Region (SAR) of China, at the nation's southernmost tip, can be divided into three parts: Hong Kong Island, the Kowloon Peninsula and the New Territories (including numerous outlying islands).

HONG KONG ISLAND

Hong Kong Island, where the earliest British settlements were established, is now dominated by futuristic buildings housing big banks and lavish hotels. Glamorous shops and restaurants rub shoulders with earthy establishments, and life moves at a breathless pace. Amid the awe-inspiring contemporary architecture, this is also the place to find some of Hong Kong's rare colonial buildings and the oldest street market in the city.

A highlight on Hong Kong Island is The Peak, home to a number of magnificent old residences. Gazing down from these rarefied heights reveals just how crowded the city below really is. Pollution and weather permitting, take in the contrasts of skyscrapers, hills and islands and the tiny size of the territory.

KOWLOON

Across the harbour from Hong Kong Island, accessible by Mass Transit Railway (MTR), Star Ferry or via one of three vehicular tunnels, Kowloon offers a taste of very urban Hong Kong, with millions of people packed into just a few square kilometres. Nathan Road is the spine of Kowloon, reaching from iconic hotel, The Peninsula, overlooking the Tsim Sha Tsui waterfront, right up towards the northern Kowloon hills, which are said to represent nine dragons *(gau lung)*, giving Kowloon its Anglicised name. In between are some of the most densely populated blocks on earth.

Tsim Sha Tsui, Kowloon's southern tip, is the traditional tourist centre of Hong Kong and the site of numerous hotels, bars and shops. It is changing as fast as anywhere in the SAR, with huge developments above and below ground.

At night there's an exciting edge to Kowloon, and while it is often referred to as gritty, it has been upping its glitz factor in recent years with new skyscrapers, malls, restaurants and a cruise terminal. It also has the city's best museums, lively outdoor markets and bargain

Capturing the classic skyline

Wong Tai Sin temple

clothing, and from Kowloon you can hop on a train to the mainland border or on a through train to Beijing and Shanghai.

THE NEW TERRITORIES AND OUTLYING ISLANDS

Beyond the mountains that ring Kowloon lie the New Territories (NT). A mix of empty hillsides, bucolic landscapes and bustling developments, they show a very different side of Hong Kong. Once defined as the land beyond Boundary Street in Kowloon and the Shenzhen River as leased by the British for 99 years in 1898, today this comprises both the land between the Kowloon hills and the Chinese border, and the outlying islands.

The New Territories are home to half of Hong Kong's population, most of whom live in purpose-built high-rise 'new towns' such as Sha Tin, alongside some traditional village housing. Much of the New Territories is made up of unpopulated grassy hills – almost half is designated country park with mountains, rugged, mangrove and sandy coastlines, and well-marked hiking trails.

Even Lantau Isand, home to the international airport and a Walt Disney theme park, is largely undeveloped and green – although new plans to develop it further were announced in early 2014.

PEOPLE

Now home to 7.2 million people, Hong Kong's population in its early years as a British colony was closer to 7,000. Since 1850, Hong Kong absorbed refugees, adventurers and entrepreneurs from all over the world, remaining predominantly Chinese. Today 95 percent of the populace is Chinese, almost half Hong-Kong born, and most have ties to southern China. There are over 300,000 foreign domestic helpers, mainly women from the Philippines and Indonesia. As many households bring in two incomes or more, many rely on live-in foreign domestic helpers to take care of their home, children and elderly relatives.

CONFUCIANISM AND CAPITALISM

Hong Kong Chinese retain traditional Confucian ideals and a strong work ethic. Buddhist and Taoist deities are actively worshipped in over 350 temples, and the various religious festivals through the year continue to outstrip their secular cousins in popularity.

Cynics like to remark that the only culture in Hong Kong is capitalism, but there is no denying conspicuous consumption and wealth have become less obvious from the late 1990s onwards, as a somewhat humbler philosophy has seeped into most walks of life

New nostalgia and confidence
Collective nostalgia, or civic pride, has recently planted itself within the city's consciousness, albeit too late to save most of the best examples of grand

On Hollywood Road

colonial-era architecture. Recent plans to level a few of the remaining privately and publicly owned structures were met with loud opposition.

A high-profile example was that of the original Star Ferry Pier in Central – a mere 50 years old, and architecturally undistinguished, but much loved. The government declared it was old enough to merit preservation (it relocated to a new Edwardian-style structure).

Heritage conservation and debates about what Hong Kong should preserve are now front-page news.The Hong Kong public, once preoccupied with securing a foreign passport, should the SAR fall apart after return to China, is confident in its future and wants to work hard and live well.

Meanwhile, the government's current tag line for Hong Kong – Asia's World City – may read a little clumsily, but it takes its cue from the official description from Beijing of the SAR as 'one country two systems'. There is space for both Confucian values and capitalism here.

HANDOVER AND BEYOND

'What has really changed since the handover?' is the perennial question from visitors to residents. Although understandable, in reality little has changed since 1997.

Normal life resumed immediately after Hong Kong's last British governor, Chris Patten, sailed off on the royal yacht in the early hours of 1 July 1997. There

were, of course, symbolic changes: the new Hong Kong Special Administrative Region flag fluttered alongside the national flag of China; the word 'Royal' was quickly removed from the institutions that bore it (except, inexplicably, from the Royal Hong Kong Yacht Club, which does fly the SAR flag); and, after old royal crests were removed, red postboxes were painted green. Streets and buildings named after ex-colonial governors and British royalty and politicians retained their original titles.

Public protests

The Hong Kong general public, though generally not highly politically motivated, takes to the street regularly when unhappy about social issues. A national holiday in celebration of the establishment of the territory as a SAR, 1 July, is one of a few days of the year that demonstrators can be relied upon to air their grievances, which currently include the absence of democratic government elections.

21st century

Despite a few political issues, Hong Kong today is undeniably optimistic. Having weathered the difficult years from 1998 to 2003, when the Asian economic crisis and two major health scares hit it hard, times are good once again. One big drag for residents is worsening air pollution, partially generated from within, but much also drifting across from industrial plants that line the SAR border in

Shooting hoops in Central

Guangdong, many of which are owned by Hong Kong companies.

For the family tourist, Hong Kong Disneyland opened in 2005, and marine-life-themed Ocean Park upped its game, with new rides and attractions and record visitor numbers – in 2007 Beijing presented it with two new pan-

DON'T LEAVE HONG KONG WITHOUT...

Trying dim sum. Hong Kong's mostly savoury dumplings bear little resemblance to versions served elsewhere. They are generally eaten for breakfast, brunch or lunch, although some establishments serve up dim sum until a little later in the afternoon. The most accessible items for those new to this kind of food are *char siu bau* (a light white bun filled with sweet chopped barbecued pork) and *har gau* (dumplings with a steamed rice flour skin, filled with seasoned shrimp and waterchestnut). See page 16.

Visiting a street market. Though there are few of these left, they recall a pre-mall sensory hustle and bustle. Besides souvenir shopping, the one in Temple Street also has some outdoor food options, from which you can still feel the atmosphere. See page 68.

Riding on the Star Ferry. Take one of two antiquated iconic forms of transport in Hong Kong (the other being a tram). Bob on Victoria Harbour and marvel at the dense cityscape set against the hills of both Kowloon and Hong Kong Island. Do this at 8pm and you will catch the nightly Symphony of Lights illuminations that bounce off buildings approximately at both ends of this short harbour hop. See page 132.

Riding on a tram. For just a few cents, take a ride through old and new neigh-bourhoods, from one end of the north shore of Hong Kong to the other, on tracks that date back to 1904. Don't be in a hurry when you ride one of these, as the speed is slow and the stops are many. In the rush hours, they are a mixed blessing: they sail through traffic jams but are jam-packed with commuters. See page 132.

Checking out its shortcuts. When the humidity and temperature rise or rainstorms hit, Hong Kongers are experts at crossing town via the elevated pedestrian walkways linking malls and office buildings. In Central and Admiralty you can walk between 40 buildings along some 7km (4 miles) of air-conditioned walkways without ever going outside. There have even been books written on the subject. Why not see how far you can get under cover?

Exploring the outlying islands. Many visitors with just a few days in Hong Kong only see the densely built downtown areas. If time allows, it's an interesting contrast to head out by ferry to an outlying island such as Lamma or Lantau. Alternatively, try a non-guided adventure on the even smaller islands of Cheung Chau or Peng Chau, both accessible from the outlying ferry piers in Central. Half a day or more in any of these will balance any view on this territory. See page 76 and 72.

A conspicuous luxury ride

das in celebration of the 10th anniversary of the handover.

Hong Kong Government and private sector celebrations in 2007 reflected that most Hong Kong residents were relatively satisfied with the life in the SAR a decade on. In the years since, property prices have spiralled, as cash-rich Mainland Chinese have snapped up a significant number of units and line up outside European brand-name stores in droves. Resentment from Hong Kong Chinese has grown, but the signature laissez-faire attitude allows this to be nothing more than a grumble.

BEYOND HONG KONG

If time allows on your visit, it's well worth exploring the area around Hong Kong. There are two key highlights: Macau and Shenzhen.

Macau
To the west of Hong Kong, across the silt-laden waters of the Pearl River Estuary (only an hour by ferry) is the once-sleepy former Portuguese enclave of Macau, rich with culture and great for food, as well as famous for being the gambling capital of Asia. Like Hong Kong, it is an SAR of China.

Shenzhen
Across the border with China proper, the city of Shenzhen is on its way to becoming one of the financial powerhouses of Asia. It makes a good day trip from Hong Kong for shopping and a taste of the People's Republic. By far the most successful of China's Special Economic Zones (SEZs), Shenzhen has grown in two decades into one of the richest cities in China. Hong Kongers still make regular trips across the border here for inexpensive recreation and bargains at its giant shopping bazaars, despite the recent strength of the Chinese renminbi (RMB).

Haggling is the order of the day at most Shenzhen shops and the cardinal rule is to bargain hard. Offer less than a third of the asking price, and settle for no more than half. Be prepared to walk away to see if the price will drop.

WHEN TO GO

Hong Kong has a humid subtropical climate, with mild winters, a warm humid spring and a stiflingly hot summer. The best time for exploring on foot is the last quarter of the year, when the humidity drops, the daytime temperatures average 24°C (75°F), and rain is rare. Winters can be chilly, with February usually the coldest month, although temperatures below 10°C (50°F) are unusual. The mercury starts rising from late March. Hong Kong tends to experience the most rain in late spring and summer. Typhoon season is June to October (direct hits are rare). Layers and an umbrella are the key to Hong Kong dressing. For more details, see www.weather.gov.hk.

Traditional pastimes   *In Nian Lin Gardens*

TOP TIPS FOR VISITING HONG KONG

Learn a little Cantonese. This is spoken as a first language by most Hong Kongers, with just under half the population now declaring that it can speak some English. Master a few simple Cantonese phrases in the Language section – see page 134.

Quality control. Look out for shops displaying a gold Q sign, which means it is a member of the Hong Kong Tourist Board's Quality Tourism Scheme. For a list of QTS-accredited outlets, pick up a copy of HKTB's *A Guide to Quality Shops*.

Explore Central on a weekday. Apart from Lan Kwai Fong/SoHo, this is not one of Hong Kong's after-hours locations – many shops close by 7pm (unlike Tsim Sha Tsui and Causeway Bay).

Cheap thrills on the Number 6 bus to Stanley. If you are travelling direct from Central to Stanley, take the No. 6 bus from Exchange Square. You'll have the best views from the top deck going over the hill along Wong Nai Chung Gap Road, and you can enjoy the white-knuckle ride down to Repulse Bay and Stanley.

Free admission to museums. Large museums, such as the Museum of History, have free admission every Wednesday.

Temple etiquette. The Chinese are generally relaxed about tourists visiting temples, but it is considered disrespectful to take pictures of people worshipping unless you have their permission.

Relax in Victoria Park. This is the largest and lushest green space in urban Hong Kong. The park is at its best in the early morning, when hundreds of tai chi devotees practise their graceful movements. The centre of the park is dominated by a statue of Queen Victoria: at Chinese New Year, she's surrounded by a giant flower market. During the mid-Autumn Festival, the park is full of families celebrating by the light of colourful lanterns – a beautiful sight. Outdoor pools offer respite from the heat, and there are tennis courts and jogging tracks. See page 37.

Hong Kong Stadium. South of Victoria Park (see page 37), this is the venue for the Hong Kong Rugby Sevens in early March. A boisterous event, it involves three days of heavy drinking, silly hats and manic singing. See www.hksevens.com for information and book well ahead, if you want to attend a particular game.

Grave matters. On one day in spring (Ching Ming) and one in autumn (Cheung Yeung) families visit cemeteries and graves to pay their respects to their ancestors. They clean the graves, make offerings and burn 'hell money', as well as gifts such as houses, phones and iPods, all made out of paper. If you want to make an offering, shops and stalls can be found just steps away from most temples.

Surfing HK. Deep Water Bay and Repulse Bay are Hong Kong's most popular and accessible beaches, but the best place is Big Wave Bay. Boards can be hired, and there are mellow places to eat and drink nearby in Shek O, one of Hong Kong island's most easy-going villages.

Classic dim sum

FOOD AND DRINK

Hong Kong, Macau and Shenzhen have thousands of places in every price range in which to eat and drink, representing almost every national and regional cuisine imaginable. Home-grown Cantonese highlights include dim sum.

Hong Kong people are passionate about eating the best possible food, whether that is a simple noodle dish or an indulgent hotel buffet. Whatever the meal, locals always have an opinion about the best places to dine. Even the most humble eatery, if good, will gain renown.

More cautious eaters should be able to find many of their favourite dishes on offer in Hong Kong, but for those who want to explore new flavours, the city will not disappoint, with its impressive range of restaurants from inexpensive to fine-dining. Adventurous and enthusiastic eaters should have a field day here.

Lunch break for many Hong Kong office workers is strictly between 1pm and 2pm, and this is by far the busiest time on the streets and in the restaurants of the business and many urban districts. Be prepared for queues, or simply avoid trying to find a table at 1pm. Go just 30 minutes earlier or later, and you'll find it much easier to get a table.

Some dining and drinking establishments have a terrace where smoking is permitted, and a few still allow it indoors; however, strict non-smoking laws apply to most.

WHERE TO EAT

Top-end restaurants

On the upscale side, there have never been so many restaurants that deliver truly gourmet dining, often in stylish surrounds, and sometimes with striking harbour views. In the past decade, many celebrity chefs have either opened a branch of their restaurants in Hong Kong – the French superchef Alain Ducasse was the first to do so with Spoon (see page 116); then came Nobu (see page 115) – or a restaurant in which they are consultant chef, as is the case with Joël Robuchon's Atelier and Pierre Gagnaire's Pierre restaurants.

Classic European fine dining in the formal sense remains in established restaurants such as the Island Shangri-La and Gaddi's (see page 113) at The Peninsula (both French) and The Verandah (Continental; see page 59) in Repulse Bay.

Fashionable restaurants

Trendy establishments in buzzing Lan Kwai Fong and SoHo – adjoining neighbourhoods in Central – serve medium-

Greens for sale   *Catching up over noodles*

to high-priced fare, as the diner is paying for the atmosphere as much as the food. Many of these places double as bars. Wan Chai also has a number of similar-style restaurant/bars.

The Kowloon equivalent is found in Knutsford Terrace and Knutsford Steps, in Tsim Sha Tsui, where there are lots of outdoor tables, spilling out from air conditioned interiors.

Nearby in Tsim Sha Tsui East there has been a mushrooming of new restaurants, many with harbour views from their terraces. Happy hours abound, with average operating hours being 5–9pm; ladies' nights allow women to either drink for free or at very reduced prices, most commonly (but not always) on a Wednesday evening. Check local publication and lifestyle website entertainment sections for a fuller picture.

WHAT TO EAT

Integral to Chinese cooking is the *yin-yang* philosophy of perfecting the correct balance of 'hot' and 'cold' ingredients. A hot *(yang)* item such as snake or chicken requires a compensating cool *(yin)* accompaniment, such as cabbage or tofu.

Cantonese food

The Cantonese typically take huge pleasure in every aspect of eating, and joke that they will eat almost anything with a spine. Indeed, people greet one another saying '*Sik fan?*' which means 'Eaten rice yet?', placing food at the heart of the culture.

At its best, Cantonese cooking is quick and light, usually steamed, blanched or stir-fried, to preserve delicate natural qualities rather than adding heavy additional flavouring. Ginger, spring onions, garlic, soy sauce and rice wine are key enhancements used sparingly, but Cantonese chefs occasionally also use strong flavours such as preserved shrimps, oyster sauce and hoisin sauce. You may initially find authentic Cantonese cuisine quite bland compared with what you've been served in Chinese restaurants abroad.

Chicken and pork are the staple meats of Cantonese fare, while duck, goose, pigeon, fish and seafood are also enjoyed – and always served at special banquets. No meal is complete without rice, either steamed or fried, or noodles – as well as tea.

Other Chinese cuisine

As well as Cantonese food you can find restaurants cooking up almost every type of Chinese cuisine in Hong Kong. From spicy Sichuan prawns and *ma po tofu* (spicy bean curd) to Mongolian hotpots and Peking duck, you can learn a lot about the diversity of China as you eat your way around the city.

Vegetarian food

There are plenty of vegetarian restaurants in Hong Kong. If you are not

Dim sum

Dim sum is a Hong Kong institution: a kind of Cantonese tapas, traditionally served from breakfast time till late lunchtime. Most common are steamed dumplings and savoury buns, rice noodles and pastries. There are scores of varieties.

Some restaurants – such as Lin Heung Tea House – still push dishes around in trolleys; ask one to stop and take a look at what's being offered, then order if you like the look of it. Most places, though, now order from menus, some with pictures.

When you are seated, order a pot of tea, and your waiter will bring you bowls, chopsticks and a card that is ticked off every time you order another bamboo basket or plate of goodies.

The most popular items appear on every dim sum menu: *har gao* are delicate steamed shrimp dumplings in translucent glutinous rice skins; *siu mai* are a colourful mix of shrimp, minced pork and diced mushroom inside yellow wonton wrappers; *cha siu bao* are big, fist-sized fluffy white buns filled with barbecued pork; *ngau yuk yuen* are steamed meatballs made with seasoned beef; and cheung fan are rolls of white rice noodle filled with meat or shrimp. You will also find deep-fried spring rolls and wonton and local favourites such as chicken's feet and sticky rice wrapped in lotus leaves.

in one, and want vegetarian food, say '*Ngoh seg choi*', and then ask for bean curd (tofu) and veggie options. Seek out Buddhist restaurants for tasty Chinese-style vegetarian food, albeit with some worryingly carnivorous-sounding dishes that are actually 'mock' meats, made of flavoured textured bean curd. Hong Kong also has numerous Indian restaurants, which are always a strong choice for vegetarian options (see below).

Indian food

The Indian community has played an important role in Hong Kong, and there are many well-established restaurants reflecting this in the city. On Hong Kong Island there are lots of good Indian restaurants around Lan Kwai Fong, SoHo and Wan Chai. In Tsim Sha Tsui, the overcrowded Chungking Mansions houses a host of small, very basic restaurants, often called 'mess clubs', specialising in inexpensive Indian, Pakistani, Afghani and Nepali food.

Out of town

The New Territories and outlying islands offer laid-back outdoor dining, often with a seafood speciality, as well as roast pigeon. Especially when the weather is fine, it is well worth stepping out of the city. Visit Sok Kwu Wan or Yung Shue Wan on Lamma Island (see page 76) for traditional alfresco dining. And if you are seeking a more international menu, Sai Kung Town, in the

Making selections at Kam Fai seafood restaurant

New Territories, has friendly restaurants on offer while on Lantau, beautiful Cheung Sha beach has South African-style food at The Stoep.

The overwhelming number of visitors to Macau may be lured by the prospect of winning at its casinos, but for the culinary adventurer a trip to Macau offers the chance to try one of the world's first fusion cuisines. Macanese food tells the former Portuguese enclave's story well: it is mainly Chinese, with elements of African and Indian spices, and hearty Portuguese ingredients and cooking methods.

Most Chinese fare here is Cantonese; some regional and international cuisine can be had. Despite the strength of the currency compared to Hong Kong, eating is cheaper. The reverse is true of drinking alcohol, which is more heavily taxed, except for local beer in modest establishments. The real top-tier restaurants are found in the best hotels.

FOOD SHOPPING

Hong Kong people like seeing their food fresh. Though avian diseases have largely curtailed sales of live poultry, you still see fish, crustacea, frogs and a few other creatures sold live at traditional 'wet markets', although nowadays these are outnumbered by supermarkets.

To see an old-style food market head to Cross Street in Wan Chai, or step off the Mid-Levels Escalator at Lyndhurst Terrace and walk down Gage Street to Graham Street. The latter market was established 160 years ago shortly after the colony of Hong Kong was founded. Hawker stalls and open-fronted shops sell an abundance of colourful fruit and vegetables, and the fish is so fresh it's flapping.

Stalls and the shops behind them sell everything from household supplies to preserved 'thousand-year-old eggs', while Chinese medicine shops – crammed full of intriguing items – add to the atmosphere.

There are plans afoot to redevelop this area into a brand-new 'Old Shop Street', so this authentic experience of Hong Kong's street life may well disappear soon.Most wet markets are now housed in functional, windowless, tiled multi-storey buildings such as Sai Ying Pun market. While not as visually appealing as old-style street markets, they nevertheless provide an insight into everyday Hong Kong food culture.

Food and Drink Prices

Throughout this guide, the following price ranges have been used to show the average cost of a three-course meal for one with a glass of wine:

$$$$ = over HK$500
$$$ = HK$300–HK500
$$ = HK$150–HK300
$ = below HK$150

Market shopping

SHOPPING

Hong Kong is known as a shopper's paradise, and its citizens (and many Chinese mainland visitors) are renowned as insatiable shoppers. Retail temptation is everywhere, from glitzy malls to bric-a-brac-packed alleys.

In Hong Kong, grand shopping malls are the main location of upmarket shops and designer brands. These mega-malls are balanced out by Hong Kong's street markets, which are lively places to shop for inexpensive clothes, gifts and souvenirs, as well as being great places for visitors to savour the sights, sounds and smells of Hong Kong life.

Most shops don't haggle, but stalls may lower their price a little and give discounts for multiple purchases. If the vendor speaks English, 'Is that your best price?' is a good starting point.

MALLS

Central's Prince's Building houses exclusive small independent shops selling antiques, jewellery and gifts for the home. Picture This on the second floor is a standout for fans of vintage posters and old maps. Neighbouring Landmark mall is swankier, and names such as Harvey Nichols, Louis Vuitton and Gucci abound. IFC mall has many fans, who flock there for its mix of expensive labels and high-street fashion brands such as Zara and Guess, plus its giant two-storey Apple store.

In Causeway Bay, Times Square also has an excellent cross-section of brands, products and price points. All electronic stores are located on the seventh and eighth floors, while fashion and footwear are spread over the third, fourth and fifth floors.

Elements is an ultramodern mall above Kowloon station, stuffed with trendy restaurants and smart shops. Close to Star Ferry in Tsim Sha Tsui, Harbour City has an extensive selection of childrenswear, a huge Toys 'R' Us toy store as well as a broad mix of fashion and lifestyle stores. Newish malls either side of Nathan Road in Tsim Sha Tsui, K11 and i-Square, reflect the 21st century in their design: lots of white space, LED lighting effects and at K11, public displays of contemporary art.

MARKETS

In Central visit The Lanes (10am–7pm), which run between Queen's Road and Des Voeux Road Central. Officially addressed Li Yuen Street East and Li Yuen Street West, these two narrow lanes are double-lined with shops and stalls selling Chinese-style clothing, cheap

The Landmark mall   *Cat Street finds*

clothes, shoes, handbags, watches and souvenirs. Between Hollywood Road and Queen's Road the stone steps of Pottinger Street are lined with stalls selling clothes, haberdashery, shoes and bargain-price fancy-dress costumes.

Stanley Market

On the south coast of Hong Kong Island, the small, covered Stanley Market (11am–6pm) is firmly geared to the tourist and a great place to buy gifts, clothes, paintings and pictures.

Kowloon's markets

In Kowloon, Temple Street Night Market (5–10pm) makes an entertaining evening, whether you are shopping or just browsing. Stalls sell a gaudy mix of souvenirs and T-shirts, trinkets, clothes and leather goods. Look out for Chinese opera singers and fortune-tellers too.

Chinese-style wares

Chinese Arts & Crafts is a reliable store for good-quality Chinese-style clothing, art, jade jewellery and gifts. You can find it at Pacific Place, 59 Queen's Road, Central, ar the China Resources Building in Wan Chai, and at Star House in Tsim Sha Tsui. For a more contemporary interpretation of the Chinese aesthetic, visit Shanghai Tang in Pedder Street Central, while GOD stores (www.god.com.hk) in several locations across the city have youthful witty takes on homeware and casual fashion.

There are food options here: street life is best enjoyed while slurping noodles from an outside stall.

Other markets nearby are good fun during the daytime: Jade Market, Flower Market, Goldfish Market and the Ladies' Market are all located just off Nathan Road and close to both Mongkok and Yau Ma Tei MTR stations.

WHAT TO BUY

Art, antiques and furniture

Hollywood Road is a good place to look for antiques and art. The Hollywood Centre at 233 Hollywood Road and nearby Cat Street Galleries have small shops within a single building. For larger items catch a taxi to Horizon Plaza, on Ap Lei Chau in the south of Hong Kong. This former industrial block has 28 floors of large warehouse-style stores including specialists in antique, reproduction and designer furniture.

Gadgets and electronics

Bargains are rare but Hong Kong is still a good place to see the latest innovations. Before paying for anything, be sure to establish whether the guarantee covers you back home. Citywide chains Fortress (www.fortress.com.hk) and Broadway are safe bets.

Keen photographers will find professional stores on Lyndhurst Terrace and Stanley Street in Central. The Wan Chai Computer Centre (130 Hennessy Road) is good for accessories.

Chinese New Year parade

ENTERTAINMENT

There's always something going on in Hong Kong, regardless of the month you visit, from traditional Chinese festivals to international arts events and fringe theatre productions.

FESTIVALS AND EVENTS

Calendar-related and arts-focussed festivals play a large part in Hong Kong's entertainment calendar. The HKTB tourist packs available at airports and border crossings – and the tourist board website (www.discover hongkong.com) – contain details on all events in town. The *South China Morning Post, HK Magazine* and *Time Out Hong Kong* all have daily and weekly updates on what's on.

Chinese New Year, also known as Spring Festival, is celebrated on the first moon of the first month of the New Year, falling in late January or early to mid-February. Businesses shut down for three days in Hong Kong, and a week on the mainland. On New Year's Day night the Hong Kong Tourist Board (HKTB) organises a parade with floats in TST; Wong Tai Sing Temple is the place to go for a traditional experience.

Other major festivals include the Bun Festival, hosted by the island of Cheung Chau – highlights include processions and the climbing of a plastic bun tower outside the Pak Tai Temple. Also notable is the Dragonboat Festival, held around Stanley, Lamma and Lantau in spring and early summer. Crews of 20 or 30 take to the water in 10m- (33ft-) long boats fronted by a dragon's head.

The annual Hong Kong Arts Festival (tel: 2824 3555; www.hk.artsfestival. org), in February and March, features top Hong Kong, Chinese artists and international performers in various venues. The City Festival (www.cityfestival.com. hk) is organised from the Fringe Club each January, with three weeks of concerts, performances, art exhibits, street events and more.

World-renowned authors come to the city in March for the Man Hong Kong International Literary Festival (www.fest ival.org.hk). Also in March – and April – is the Hong Kong International Film Festival (www.hkiff.org.hk), while Hong Kong Art Walk, a tour of commercial galleries (drinks and canapés served), is every March or April. Le French May (www.le frenchmay.com) extends to summer and promotes all kinds of arts with a French connection.

THEATRE AND DANCE

Most local theatre productions are in Cantonese, though some of the larger

Chinese opera　　　　　　　　　　　　*Dragonboat Festival*

venues run English and Mandarin subtitles. Hong Kong Repertory Theatre (www.hkrep.com) produces Chinese and international drama, in Cantonese with English subtitles.

Hong Kong has a vibrant dance scene and a number of dance companies in permanent residence. Hong Kong Dance Company (www.hkdance.com) draws on Hong Kong's cultural mix, performing traditional folk dance, dance drama, and original works incorporating Western techniques. City Contemporary Dance Company (www.ccdc.com.hk) is Hong Kong's leading modern dance company, while Hong Kong Ballet (www.hkballet.com) is one of the foremost classical ballet companies in Asia.

MUSIC

The Hong Kong Philharmonic Orchestra (HKPO; www.hkpo.com), one of Asia's leading orchestras, presents over 150 performances each year, from core symphonic classics to collaboration with artists of Canto-pop (a type of saccharine pop music). The HKPO Hong Kong Sinfonietta (www.hksinfonietta.org) performs over 70 times a year, and is renowned for its innovative audience development concerts, crossover productions and new commissions.

It's not all classical, though. Scratch under the surface and Hong Kong's live music scene is there to be found. Starting points for investigating the underground music scene are venues such as Rockschool (see page 119) and the Fringe Club (see page 118). Underground HK (www.undergroundhk.com) and Shazza Music (www.shazzamusic.com) promote independent artists.

Canto-pop is hugely popular in Hong Kong. Big names include teen idols Eason Chan, and Twins.

FILM

Hong Kong is not making as many movies as it once did, but its global influence is widely recognised thanks to the Hollywood success of director John Woo, actors Michelle Yeow, Chow Yun-fat and the irrepressible Jackie Chan. Oscar wins for Martin Scorsese's remake of Andrew Lau and Alan Mak's Hong Kong crime-thriller *Infernal Affairs*, kung-fu epic *Crouching Tiger, Hidden Dragon* (a joint production between Hong Kong, mainland China, Taiwan and the US), plus the enduring popularity of Bruce Lee, all sustain the city's movie industry.

NIGHTLIFE

Hong Kong Island's nightlife is largely centred around Lan Kwai Fong, Wyndham Steet and SoHo in Central and Wan Chai, while Sheung Wan and Kennedy Town have a few new spots. In Kowloon, TST and TST East many venues have outdoor seating and harbour views that are popular with visitors and locals alike. For further recommendations, see the Nightlife section (see page 118).

HISTORY: KEY DATES

Initially regarded by the British as an ill-chosen gain of limited value, Hong Kong became an important part of the Empire and was reluctantly relinquished. The city is now thriving as a Special Administrative Region, under Chinese rule.

EARLY HISTORY

*c.*4000 BC	Aborigines set up Stone-Age settlements in coastal areas.
AD 1577	Portugal establishes official trading colony at Macau.
1662	Imperial edict aimed at quelling rebels and pirates forces coastal dwellers to uproot and move inland.
1669	Evacuation edict is reversed, and coastal areas are repopulated by Hakka people from northern China.
1714	Canton (Guangzhou) opened to foreign trade; the British East India Company (EIC) is established.
1799	China bans the opium trade, but the lucrative drug, used as trading currency, continues to be smuggled.
1839	Commissioner Lin Tse-hu confiscates more than 20,000 chests of opium from British traders, sparking off the First Opium War.
1841	Britain takes unofficial possession of Hong Kong Island.

COLONIAL PERIOD

1842	Hong Kong Island is officially ceded to Britain (Treaty of Nanking).
1860	Kowloon Peninsula and Stonecutters Island are ceded to Britain as part of the Convention of Peking following the Second Opium War.
1898	Britain negotiates a 99-year lease of the New Territories and Outlying Islands.
1938	Canton falls to Japan. Refugees flee to Hong Kong.
1941	Hong Kong falls to invading Japanese on Christmas Day.
1945	World War II ends. Hong Kong is liberated on 30 August.
1949–53	Communist victory on mainland China sees massive waves of refugees swell the local population. Industrialisation commences.
1954	Government initiates public-housing programmes, following the mushrooming of unsanitary squatter settlements.

Victoria Port in 1850

1966–7	Pro-Communist riots inspired by the Cultural Revolution in China.
1973	First of several New Towns opened in Tuen Mun, New Territories.
1979	Mass Transit Railway (MTR) opens.
1984	Margaret Thatcher and Chinese premier Zhao Ziyang sign a declaration for Hong Kong to revert to Chinese rule in 1997.
1992	Governor Chris Patten appointed the last British colonial head.
1995	A fully elected Legislative Council (LegCo) is voted into power as part of Patten's push for more democracy.

HANDOVER AND BEYOND

1997	China resumes sovereignty, Tung Chee-hwa appointed Chief Executive of the Hong Kong Special Administrative Region (SAR), as LegCo is briefly replaced by Provisional Legislature.
1998	Elections held for LegCo. New airport opens at Chek Lap Kok. The Hong Kong Stock Market dives as the Asian economic crisis grips. Avian flu emerges.
1999	Rule of law is undermined, as government asks Beijing to overturn Court of Final Appeal's ruling on the right of abode.
2000	Elections for second four-year term of office for LegCo.
2002	Tung Chee-hwa made Chief Executive for second five-year term.
2003	Hong Kong struggles with a weak economy; 299 people killed by the SARS virus. On 1 July over 500,000 people march against Article 23, an anti-subversion bill.
2004	Beijing rules out universal suffrage by 2007.
2005	Civil servant Donald Tsang made second HKSAR Chief Executive.
2006	China booms, and Hong Kong economy surges. 25.25 million people visit Hong Kong; 13 million are tourists from the mainland.
2007	Donald Tsang re-elected. HKSAR celebrates 10th anniversary.
2008	Hong Kong hosts equestrian events for Beijing 2008 Olympics.
2009	Consumer and business confidence returns to pre-recession levels.
2010	Five LegCo members resign to pressure Beijing for full democracy.
2012	Leung Chun-ying assumes office as the third SAR Chief Executive. Mainland Chinese visitor numbers of 34.9 million account for 71.8 per cent from outside of Hong Kong.
2013	Total visitor arrivals rise further, with nearly 52.3 million visitors.

BEST ROUTES

CENTRAL DISTRICT

After breakfast at an IFC or Exchange Square café, explore Central and its awe-inspiring modern architecture, St John's Cathedral and the Zoological and Botanical Gardens. Take the Peak Tram up to the Peak and stop for lunch, then head back via Hong Kong Park, Flagstaff House and another tram ride.

DISTANCE: 5km (3 miles)
TIME: Half to a full day
START: Hong Kong Airport Express Station, Exit B2
END: Central Ferry Piers 7 and 8
POINTS TO NOTE: This is mainly a walking route, with trips on the Peak Tram and a double-decker city tram to cover longer or steeper sections and to add variety.

This route is designed to give you a feel for Central District, the hub of wealth and power in Hong Kong since the British first took possession of this barren rock on the coast of China in 1841. This is a route ideally followed on a weekday, so that you can get a sense of the buzz of the business and financial centre in full swing.

On Sundays and public holidays thousands of predominantly Filipina domestic helpers, enjoying their only time off, gather to picnic and socialise on Central's walkways and squares, which makes for a festive atmosphere.

EXCHANGE SQUARE

From the Hong Kong terminus of the Airport Express line, take the elevator to Level One and walk through IFC Mall (see below) to **Exchange Square** ❶, home to the Hong Kong Stock Exchange. You can stop for breakfast at one of the many coffee shops in the IFC, such as **Open Kitchen**, see ❶ or **TWG Tea**, see ❷. If you're early enough at the latter, you might see people practising tai chi through its windows, outside Exchange Square. Otherwise, breakfast while enjoying the people-watching and then admire the large bronze sculptures here: *Tai Chi* by Ju Ming, Henry Moore's *Oval with Points* and the life-size *Water Buffalo* by Dame Elisabeth Frink.

Two IFC
Looming largest of all above the three towers of Exchange Square and the vast International Finance Centre (IFC) is Hong Kong's second-tallest building, **Two IFC** ❷. Completed in 2003, at 415m (1,362ft) it is one the top-20 tall-

A nightime view of Central

est buildings in the world – currently, at least. IFC includes the Hong Kong MTR and Airport Express Station, the One and Two IFC office towers. IFC Mall has hundreds of shops, a cosy cinema and dozens of cafés and restaurants with wonderful views of the harbour.

POWERHOUSES

Now follow the elevated walkway east beyond One Exchange Square and take the second bridge on the right across Connaught Road, then through Chater House. Make your way down to street

Map

200 m / 220 yds

Peak Tower — 10
Peak Galleria — 5
Findlay Road
Peak Tram
Barker Road
Peak Tram Terminus

Central Ferry Piers (Star Ferry) — 15
Hong Kong Maritime Museum — 16
Pier 6, Pier 7, Pier 8, Pier 9, Pier 10
Man Kwong Street

Victoria Harbour

Des Voeux Road
Connaught Road
The Center
Jubilee St
Q. Victoria St
Des Voeux St
Douglas St
Douglas Lane
Pottinger St
Central Market
Cochrane St
Wellington Street
Stanley Street
Aroundnot
Wyndham Street
Zetland St
Glenealy

ifc Mall — 1
Finance St
Airport Express
Two ifc — 2
Two ifc
International Finance Centre (ifc) — 2
Hong Kong
Man Cheung St
Harbour View St
The Forum
Exchange Square — 1
Man Yiu Street
Connaught Pl
General Post Office
Jardine House
Pedder St Tunnel
World Wide House
Chater House
Central
Pedder St
Mandarin Oriental Hong Kong
Prince's Building
Ice House St
Theatre La
Chater Road
Central
STATUE — 3
SQUARE — 4
Des Voeux Rd
Former Supreme Court Building — 5
HSBC HQ Building — 6
Queen's Rd C.
Battery Path
Dairy Farm Building
Fringe Club — 8
Duddell St
Ice House St
Lan Kwai Tong
Wyndham St
Upper Albert Road
Caritas Centre
Government House
Glenealy
ZOOLOGICAL AND BOTANICAL GARDENS — 9
Robinson Rd
Albany Rd
Cotton Tree Dr.
Peak Tram
Peak Tower

General Post Office
CENTRAL
Lung Wo Road
CENTRAL AND WESTERN DISTRICT PROMENADE (under construction)
Central Wan Chai Bypass
Edinburgh Place
City Hall
Central Barracks
T A M A R
TAMAR PARK
AIG Tower
Hong Kong Club Road
Central Road
Central Government Complex
Lambeth Walk
Harcourt Road
Murray Rd
CHATER GARDEN
Bank of China — 14
Fairmont House
Cheung Kong Center
Bank of China Tower
Cotton Tree Drive
Queensway Plaza
Tim Wa Avenue
Admiralty
Queensway Plaza
Court of Final Appeal
Citibank Plaza ICBC Tower — 7
St John's Cathedral
Cotton Tree Drive
Flagstaff House Museum of Tea Ware — 12
Queensway
Peak Tram Terminus
Garden Rd
HONG KONG PARK — 11
Supreme Court Rd
Island Shangri-La — 13
Pacific Place
Conrad

Some of Central's important buildings

level, turn left down Chater Road and walk towards the **Mandarin Oriental Hong Kong ❸** hotel.

Opened in 1963, this flagship hotel of the luxury chain is home to Hong Kong institutions such as the Captain's Bar and the Mandarin Grill, long favoured by movers and shakers. Rose-petal jam or handmade chocolates from the Mandarin Cake Shop make great gifts.

Cross the road to **Statue Square ❹**, so-called because it originally housed statues of Queen Victoria, Prince Albert and Edward VII when it opened in 1902.

LegCo and the Club

The Neoclassical **Former Supreme Court Building ❺**, on the east side of Statue Square, was built in 1912. From 1985 it was home to Hong Kong's governing body, the Legislative Council (LegCo), which has now moved to the Legislative Council Complex, next to the new Central Government Headquarters, completed in 2011. Alongside this tree-lined structure are the cenotaph, commemorating the dead of World War I, and the Chater Gardens. Overlooking all this is the city's exclusive Hong Kong Club, in a building of the same name (1980) by the Australian architect Harry Seidler.

The only statue in the square is that of banker Sir Thomas Jackson, one of the foremost early managers of the Hongkong and Shanghai Banking Corporation (HSBC), which opened its first

headquarters across the road to the south of the square in 1865.

'The Bank'

Cross Des Voeux Road to explore the **HSBC Headquarters Building ❻**. Designed in 1985 by the British architect Norman Foster, it is viewed as one of the world's most innovative structures, due to its exo-skeleton and lack of internal support. Pass the two bronze lions that guard the front of the building, looking out for bullet marks on 'Stephen', the left-hand one (the other is called Sitt), from the Battle of Hong Kong (1941). Walk underneath the bank and gaze up at the building's 'guts' through the glass floor. During banking hours you can take an escalator up to the main public hall on level 3 for a closer look.

Afterwards, continue heading inland, away from the harbour, across the footbridge over Queen's Road Central to Battery Path.

COLONIAL REMINDERS

Once over the bridge, turn left up banyan-shaded Battery Path, past the red-brick Court of Final Appeal Building (closed to visitors), dating from 1917 and also known as the Former French Mission Building, to **St John's Cathedral ❼** (daily 7am–6pm). Dwarfed by the cathedrals of commerce all around it, this fine Victorian Gothic building was consecrated in 1849. Pause for a

Pedestrian walkways　　　　　　　　　　　　　　　　*St John's Cathedral*

moment to take in the peaceful interior, with its turquoise timber ceiling and gently whirring fans. There are views across its small garden to the soaring Bank of China building nearby.

From here, either take a footbridge across Garden Road to the Peak Tram terminus or take a detour around some more colonial sites.

Hilly Hong Kong

To continue the tour, return to Queen's Road Central down Battery Path, then take the second left into Duddell Street, climbing the steps at its far end. The quaint gas lamps at the top and bottom of the steps are more than 100 years old and are the only ones still in active service in Hong Kong.

At this point, turn right to follow the curve of Ice House Street, past a cluster of old colonial buildings. Straight ahead is the red-brick **Dairy Farm Building**, built as an ice house in the late 19th century and first restored in 1913. It now houses both the members-only Foreign Correspondents' Club and Hong Kong's foremost alternative arts venue, the **Fringe Club** ❽, which hosts exhibitions, music, theatre and performances and has restaurants and bars next to its roof garden and in its basement, see ❸.

To the left are Bishop's House (1850) and St Paul's Episcopal Church (1911). Lan Kwai Fong and Wyndham Street (see page 45), with their plethora of restaurants open from lunchtime onwards, are just around the corner.

Zoo and Botanical Gardens

Head up Glenealy, veering right at the appropriate sign through a pedestrian subway. Turn left opposite the Caritas Centre into the **Hong Kong Zoological and Botanical Gardens** ❾ (daily 6am–7pm). The zoo is tiny and old-fashioned by international standards, but the botanical gardens (est. 1864) offer a pleasant green retreat from the hectic city.

Exit from the gardens' eastern end and negotiate your way across the Upper Albert Road junction by two flights of steps. Take a slight detour left along Upper Albert Road to view the front of Government House (1855), which was the official residence of 25 of Hong Kong's 28 British Governors. From 2004 until 2012 it was also the home of the HKSAR's second Chief Executive, Donald Tsang; his successor chose not to live there.

Now retrace your steps along Upper Albert Road across Garden Road and follow the signs to Hong Kong Park and the Peak Tram station, under the Cotton Tree Drive flyover.

UP TO THE PEAK

In continuous operation since 1888, the Peak Tram is actually a funicular railway, built to serve the wealthy residents of The Peak who previously had to rely on human-carried sedan chairs for transport to the waterfront. Trams depart every 10 to 15 minutes from

Riding the Peak Tram

7am to midnight for an exhilarating journey to the summit.

Exit at the **Peak Tower** ⑩ and head up the escalators to the rooftop **Sky Terrace** (charge). The 360-degree panoramic views from the top are magnificent on a clear day. You can stop for lunch at any of the Peak Tower's restaurants and cafés (see page 109), or try Café Deco in the Peak Galleria or the **Peak Lookout** (see page 109), across the road. For a longer exploration of the Peak, see page 54.

Down to Hong Kong Park

Return downhill on the Peak Tram. Exit the station, and turn right under the

> ## HK skyline
>
> Seen from the top of the Peak or the Star Ferry, Hong Kong's rocketing skyline is awe inspiring. Two prime landmarks, the HSBC and Bank of China, date from the 1980s, while its biggest tower, Two IFC, was completed in 2004. On the Kowloon side building was long restricted by the proximity of Kai Tak airport, but since the new airport opened in 1998 this area has become a developers' playground. The tallest building in the city is the 118-storey International Commerce Centre (ICC), 480m (1,588ft) above Kowloon station and surrounded by a cluster of high-end high-rise residential towers topping 200m (660ft).

Cotton Tree Drive flyover into **Hong Kong Park** ⑪ (daily 6am–11pm). Wander round the high-tech aviary and greenhouses, see couples posing for photos in full wedding regalia by the registry office, or climb the 105 steps of the observatory tower for another sweeping view. Another reason to come here is to visit the **Flagstaff House Museum of Tea Ware** ⑫ (Wed–Mon 10am–5pm). Constructed in 1846, the house is the oldest European structure still standing in Hong Kong. It served as the residence of the Commander-in-Chief of the British Forces for more than 130 years, but now hosts intriguing exhibits on everything to do with tea and it also has a nice tearoom.

MODERN SPIRES

Leave the park by the Supreme Court Road exit. Take the elevator on your left down to **Pacific Place** ⑬, a vast hotel and shopping complex that also has enjoyable places to eat, such as **Peking Garden**, see ❹. If you're not in the mood for shopping, follow the signs for Admiralty MTR station and Queensway Plaza, reached via a pedestrian bridge over Queensway. Halfway across, take the steps down to the tramway and ride three stops on a westbound tram.

High finance

The first stop takes you as far as the **Bank of China** ⑭ (1989), an eye-

catching prism-like structure designed by Sino-American architect I.M. Pei and, standing at 70 storeys (367m/1,204ft). Next door is the 283m (927-ft) high Cheung Kong Centre (1999).

Chater Garden opposite, once home of the exclusive Hong Kong Cricket Club, is now a pleasant urban open space. The tramline wraps around the Art Deco-style old Bank of China Building (1950), and stops outside the HSBC headquarters at Statue Square. Squeeze your way to the front of the tram to pay your fare, so you can get off at the next stop.

Disembark at World Wide House, then head towards the harbour along Pedder Street via the footbridge across four-lane Connaught Road. Pass Jardine House and the General Post Office to your right and follow the walkway to the waterfront. To your left is IFC; to the right look over reclaimed land towards Wan Chai. From here you can see your final destination, the Edwardian-style **Central Ferry Pier** ⑮ (2006). Catch a Star Ferry across to Kowloon from pier 7, and get a full view of the Hong Kong skyline. If time allows, check out the newly positioned Hong Kong Maritime Museum ⑯ at pier 8.

Food and Drink

① OPEN KITCHEN

Podium level 1, IFC Mall; tel: 2234 7356; $–$$

Top coffee plus pastries and sandwiches to take away or eat in. It's hard not to stay though, as the whole of one side is floor-to-ceiling picture windows facing the harbour.

② TWG TEA SALON AND BOUTIQUE IFC

Podium level 1, IFC Mall; tel: 2796 2828; $$–$$$

This upscale Singaporean tea room's first foray into Hong Kong offers four types of refined Western breakfasts from $160 from 10–11.30am.

③ FRINGE CLUB

2 Lower Albert Road, Central; tel: 2521

7251; $–$$

A good place to stop for a refreshing beverage any time from noon to midnight. Its two cosy restaurant-cum-bars were relaunched in January 2014. Colette's, adjoining the rooftop garden has a vegetarian lunch buffet Mon–Fri noon–2.30pm. The main ground floor café and bar The Vault serves healthy salads, sandwiches and some hot dishes, alongside hot drinks and interesting wines and beers and is also a venue for exhibitions and live music (see page 118).

④ PEKING GARDEN

Shop 005, Pacific Place; tel: 2845 8452; $$

Lively restaurant offering northern Chinese food. Peking duck carving exhibitions are a speciality.

Dried sausage on Queen's Road West

WESTERN DISTRICT

This route reveals two contrasting atmospheres: the calm campus of Hong Kong University and then the tightly packed, oldest Chinese districts of Sai Ying Pun and Sheung Wan, with their constant street life and fascinating shops.

DISTANCE: 3km (2 miles)
TIME: Half a day
START: HK University
END: Sheung Wan MTR
POINTS TO NOTE: The best way to use this route is as a base for wandering and exploring the alleys and sidestreets of these residential and trading districts. The route is flat apart from the steep walk downhill along Centre Street.

This route concentrates on one of the oldest, least-modernised parts of Hong Kong, the atmospheric streets of Sai Ying Pun and Sheung Wan, west of Central. Less hectic than Kowloon, this is everyday Hong Kong street life, where open-fronted 'shop-houses' and family businesses, not mega malls and brands, set the tone. Along the main streets, goods from the trading houses and shops overflow onto pavements with a mix of everything from daily necessities to traditional Chinese medicine, 'hell money' and dim sum baskets.

Start on a more relaxed note, though, at the campus of Hong Kong University (HKU) in Pok Fu Lam. Take a 3A, 7 or 91 bus from the Central Ferry Pier bus terminal and get off on Pok Fu Lam Road when you see the sign for Hong Kong University, and (on your right) the modern Haking Wong Building.

THE UNIVERSITY

Founded at the start of the 20th century, **Hong Kong University** ❶ is now one of Asia's leading academic institutions, with 10,000 students. Enter the campus at the West Gate on Pok Fu Lam Road, with steps leading up to the Haking Wong Building on your right. Turn left to enter the original campus, beneath shady trees.

To the right, the Main Arts Building is a stately Edwardian structure dating to 1910 with internal courtyards and graceful palms. Across the path the graceful Hung Hing Ying Building, constructed in 1919, houses the Music Department (open to the public for recitals).

Tea in Sheung Wan　　　　　　　　　*A tailor at work*

University Museum and Art Gallery

Follow the driveway round to Bonham Road and the **University Museum and Art Gallery** ② (www.hkumag.hku.hk; Mon–Sat 9.30am–6pm, Sun 1.30–5.30pm). The 1930s Fung Ping Shan Building contains a diverse collection of early Chinese bronzes, ceramics and other artefacts, including a unique set of bronze crosses made by the Nestorians, a Christian community who have lived in China since around AD 600. There are also fine Ming and early Qing paintings, while contemporary Chinese art is exhibited in the TT Tsui Building alongside, linked by a footbridge. Pause to enjoy some Chinese tea at the museum's **Tea Gallery**, see ①.

SAI YING PUN

Leaving the University, head back eastwards on Bonham Road, and shortly after the grey columns and the brick of King's College School, which was founded in 1926, turn left down pedestrianised **Centre Street** ③. This area is called Sai Ying Pun: *Sai* means west, *Ying Pun* means military camp, and this was where the first British camps were established in the 1840s.

The section below High Street is clinging to a flavour of an older Hong Kong, with small earth god shrines outside each shop, even though modern indoor markets have replaced outdoor stalls along the steep street.

But the new pedestrian escalator that runs up Centre Street from First Street and an MTR station due to open in 2014 is bringing inevitable change. Cafés, galleries and trendier boutiques are beginning to grace the vicinity. Locals still shop at **Sai Ying Pun Market**, though, at the junction of Centre and Second for meat, fish and vegetables.

As you walk down Centre Street you cross Third, Second and First streets until you reach **Queen's Road**, the first road built in Hong Kong after the British claimed the island in 1841.

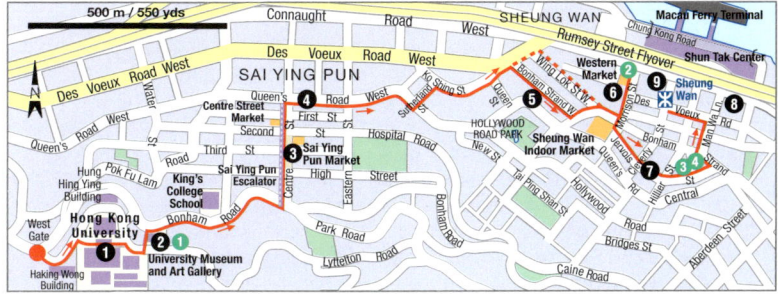

Dried chillis

FUNERAL SHOPPING

Turn right at the corner – past a Cantonese-style cooked meat shop – onto **Queen's Road West** ❹, and then walk for a few minutes to reach a row of shops on the right selling floral wreaths, joss sticks, sacks of 'hell' money, other paper offerings and brass urns – everything you need for a traditional Chinese funeral can be found here except for coffins, which are supplied by shops nearby on Hollywood Road. Keeping up with the times, paper items for the afterlife now include speedboats, mobile phones and flat-screen televisions.

SHEUNG WAN BAZAAR

Cross Queen's Road West and cut down Sutherland Street and turn right along Ko Shing Street. Browse the shops selling traditional Chinese medicines, dried foods, shrimps, starfish and tubs of exotic-looking items, and take in their pungent aromas.

Continue on Des Voeux Road West to reach, on your right, **Bonham Strand West** ❺, where the shops deal wholesale in items prized in traditional Chinese medicine and cuisine – ginseng, antelope horn, birds' nests and abalone. This area is also at the centre of the controversial global trade in shark fin. Once a regional delicacy eaten only occasionally, it is now extremely popular throughout the country.

Western Market

Heading back towards Central, cross **Sheung Wan Fong**, a busy little piazza. On your right is a 12-storey civic centre housing a wet market and leisure facilities.

Head left down On Tai Street, past stalls selling dried food, takeaway noodles, and fruit and vegetables, to reach **Western Market** ❻, built in 1906. Used as a fresh produce market for more than 80 years, this handsome, European-looking, red-brick building was restored in 1991 as a period shopping mall, retaining its elegant architectural features. You'll find interesting memorabilia, handicrafts, toys, jewellery and other gifts on the ground floor, and fabric merchants selling everything from Chinese silk to Harris Tweed upstairs. Prices are fair, and the merchants know their stuff. Upstairs is the **Grand Stage**, see ❷, enlivened by afternoon 'tea dances'.

The heart of Sheung Wan

Go back up Morrison Street to explore **Sheung Wan** further. Turn left into **Jervois Street** ❼, which marked the waterfront until the first harbour reclamation began in 1852; signs for ships' chandlers remind you of the area's past.

Cleverly Street has a shady outdoor seating area next to a caged-bird shop. Local bird fanciers gather here with their prized possessions. At 13 Hillier Street is one of Hong Kong's fabled reptile

Traditional Chinese medicines   *In Chop Market*

shops. Snakes are considered a win-
tertime delicacy, as the meat and body
fluids are believed to fortify the human
body against the cold; geckos, on the
other hand, are served on the menu all
year round.

Shops that have been selling rice,
herbs, specialist teas, noodles, preserved fruits and Chinese sweets for 60
to 100 years are interspersed with the
more everyday shops selling hardware,
fruit and flowers, as well as a posh
French delicatessen (Monsieur Chatté,
121 Bonham Strand). There are some
good inexpensive cafés and restaurants serving the local office workers
around here, see ❸ and ❹, and also
Tim's Kitchen (see page 110).

Chop Alley

At the end of Jervois Street turn left back
onto Bonham Strand. Turn right after
a branch of the HSBC bank, into **Man
Wa Lane** ❽, known as 'Chop Alley'.
Chop-makers have been plying their
trade here since the 1920s, carving traditional Chinese seals or 'chops' from
stone, jade, bone or ivory; the art itself
is some 3,000 years old. Chop-makers
will translate your name and carve a
custom chop in one to four hours.

Turn left on Wing Lok Street for **Sheung
Wan MTR station** ❾; alternatively, follow
the lane to Des Voeux Road and hop on
a tram, or wander slowly east along Des
Voeux Road, exploring yet more narrow
lanes that connect it to Queen's Road.

Food and Drink

❶ TEA GALLERY
University Museum and Art Gallery, TT Tsui
Building, 94 Bonham Road; $
Tea is served in miniature pots and porcelain
cups at four traditional rosewood tables
on the gallery's lower floor. Novices are
encouraged to brew up themselves: a 'how-
to' guide is provided.

❷ THE GRAND STAGE
2/F Western Market, 23 Des Voeux Road,
Sheung Wan; tel: 2815 2311; $$
This old-world restaurant on the top floor of
Western Market serves familiar dim sum and
Cantonese favourites.

❸ MALAY MAMA
11A Mercer Street, Sheung Wan; tel: 2542
4111; $
Noodle fans pack into this no-frills
Malaysian café that specialises in hearty
bowls of Laksa, Ipoh Ho Fun and Prawn
Mee.

❹ MASALA
10 Mercer Street, Sheung Wan; tel: 2581
9777; $
This friendly Indian restaurant offers a
wide choice of dishes at inexpensive
prices. Standouts include bhindi masala,
fish madras, tarka dhal and tandoori
chicken. Also does excellent-value set
menus.

Commuter heading for Happy Valley

CAUSEWAY BAY AND HAPPY VALLEY

Causeway Bay is the busiest of all Hong Kong's shopping hubs, packed with malls, stores and cafés. This route explores its other attractions, including the green space of Victoria Park and Hong Kong's favourite sport – horse-racing.

DISTANCE: 5km (3 miles)
TIME: Half a day
START: Causeway Bay MTR
END: Happy Valley Racecourse
POINTS TO NOTE: Start around 11.30am, to be in time to catch the midday gun. Take the MTR to Causeway Bay (Exit E) and head to the waterfront.

NOON-DAY GUN

The practice of firing a cannon at the stroke of noon was begun by Jardine, Matheson & Co after they set up their trading base at Causeway Bay in the 1840s. Legend has it that Jardine's firing of the gun to salute its managers whenever they returned to Hong Kong annoyed the colonial government, and they were ordered to fire it every day as a punishment. Jardine moved long ago to Central, but still runs the gun, with the Scottish flag of its founders alongside the Bauhinia, a quaint daily reminder of the area's colourful merchant history.

To witness this quaint reminder of the area's colourful merchant history, make sure you are at Exit E of Causeway Bay MTR station or outside Sogo Department store by 11.30am. Head north towards the harbour along East Point Road, then cut through to the east side of the World Trade Centre. Look out for the entrance to the Centre's underground car park, and signs for the Noon Day Gun. These will lead you under the main road through the car park, a route shared with the Police Officers' Club and the Royal Hong Kong Yacht Club. Emerge into the daylight beside the harbour, and you'll see a small garden containing the celebrated **Noon-Day Gun ❶**. As you wait for the brief ceremony of firing the gun, take in the view of Kowloon and the contrasts of **Causeway Bay Typhoon Shelter**, which houses a mixed bag of yacht club members' luxury cruisers, rickety wooden junks and sampans. This area of water will be reclaimed temporarily during the construction of the Central-Wan Chai bypass and returned to the community in 2020.

Punters at the races   *In Causeway Bay*

VICTORIA PARK AND TIN HAU

After the big bang, wander east along the waterfront and cross to **Victoria Park ❷**, the city's largest urban green space, and wander down to its southeast corner. This area, known as **Tin Hau** and part of North Point district, had a massive influx of residents and businesses from Shanghai in the 1950s.

At the eastern side of the park, perched on a granite ledge that once overlooked the original Causeway Bay, is the 18th-century **Tin Hau Temple ❸** (daily 7am–5pm), the best known of more than 100 temples around the Territory dedicated to the Daoist Queen of Heaven, goddess of the sea and protector of seafarers.

Lin Fa Kung Temple

Walk back down Tin Hau Temple Road and turn left into Tung Lo Wan Road to reach **Lin Fa Kung Temple ❹** (daily 7.30am–5pm), set back down a lane. Dating from 1864, but renovated in 1999, it is dedicated to the Goddess of Mercy, and consists of an octagonal structure straddling a giant boulder, making it one of Hong Kong's most unusual Buddhist shrines. Inside, there's a main shrine, and a turtle pool. During the Mid-Autumn Festival (September), some one hundred men carry a 'dragon' of smoking joss sticks through these streets.

Central Library

Return to Tung Lo Wan Road, and carry on round towards the back of the sand-yellow **Central Library ❺**. Behind its Neoclassical façade is a modern 10-storey facility, with free internet access, over 4,000 journals from around the world, and the territory's best historical reference books.

CAUSEWAY BAY SHOPPING

It's now time to explore the area with some of the most expensive retail space on the planet – but still with bargains to find. From the library, follow Tung Lo Wan Road to Leighton Road, and take the footbridge across it to Irving Street and the start of **Jardine's Bazaar ❻**, so-called because it was once a popular clothes market, although it now has a more standard mix of shops and cafés.

Mall life

At the end of the bazaar turn left on Kai Chiu Road to Lee Garden Road, home to bargain factory-outlet clothing shops, then cross Percival Street and its tramlines to **Times Square ❼**, one of the area's most varied high-rise malls, with its own MTR entrance and some good restaurants in the **Food Forum** on the upper floors, where you can end the tour, break for lunch, or ride the bubble lift up to see the urban view.

Mall dining is a very fashionable part of the Hong Kong lifestyle, and has to be tried at least once. **Zushi ANA**, see

The course by night

, and **Heichinrou**, see , are just two of several options; for something more laid-back, head down to the basement food court and the **City'super Cooked Deli**, see .

TRAM RIDE

After lunch, hop on a tram going south along Percival Street; get a seat upstairs to make the most of the view. As the

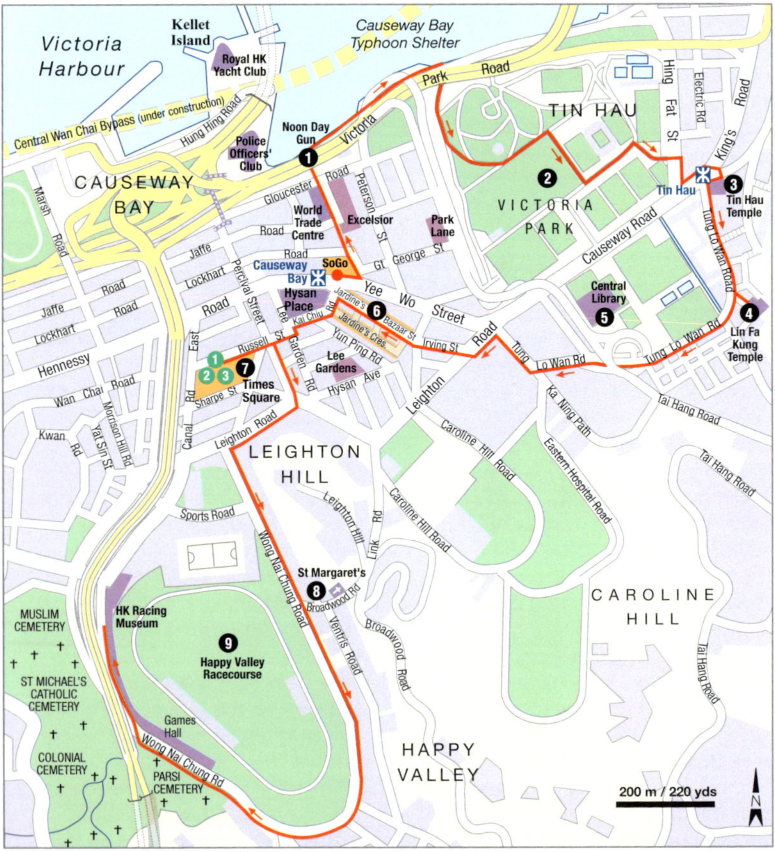

Victoria Harbour

Kellet Island

Royal HK Yacht Club

Causeway Bay Typhoon Shelter

Park Road

Central Wan Chai Bypass (under construction)

Hung Hing Road

Noon Day Gun

TIN HAU

Hing Fat St.

Electric Rd.

King's Rd.

Police Officers' Club

Victoria Road

Gloucester Road

CAUSEWAY BAY

Marsh Road

Jaffe Road

World Trade Centre

Paterson St.

Excelsior

Road

Park Lane

VICTORIA PARK

Tin Hau

Tin Hau Temple

Causeway Bay

SoGo

Gt. George St.

Yee Wo Street

Causeway Road

Central Library

Tung Lo Wan Rd.

Lin Fa Kung Temple

Lockhart Road

Jaffe Road

Hysan Place

Jardine's Bazaar St.

Jardine's Cres.

Irving St.

Tung Lo Wan Rd.

Percival Street

Pak Sha Rd.

Yun Ping Rd.

Lee Gardens

Hysan Ave.

Tung Lo Wan Rd.

Hennessy

Lockhart Road

Russell St.

Sharp St. East

Canal Road

Times Square

Leighton

Leighton Road

Ka Ning Path

Tai Hang Road

Wan Chai Road

Morrison Hill St.

Yat Sin St.

Kwan

Leighton Road

Caroline Hill Road

Eastern Hospital Road

Tai Hang Road

LEIGHTON HILL

Sports Road

Wong Nai Chung Road

Leighton Hill Rd.

Caroline Hill Road

St Margaret's

Broadwood Rd.

Venturi Road

Broadwood Road

CAROLINE HILL

MUSLIM CEMETERY

HK Racing Museum

Happy Valley Racecourse

ST MICHAEL'S CATHOLIC CEMETERY

COLONIAL CEMETERY

Games Hall

Wong Nai Chung Rd.

PARSI CEMETERY

HAPPY VALLEY

200 m / 220 yds

N

Racing to the last

tram rumbles along Wong Nai Chung Road, notice the elegant façade of **St Margaret's Church** ❽, perched up the hill on the left, and Happy Valley Racecourse on your right. From the end of the line, walk down along the west side of the racecourse.

HAPPY VALLEY

Happy Valley was mosquito-ridden marshland until the 1840s, when it was reclaimed by the British first for cemeteries and then, from 1846, as the spot for Hong Kong's racetrack. These days the atmosphere inside and outside the **Happy Valley Racecourse** ❾ for the Wednesday evening races (Sept–Jun) is electric; Hong Kongers love to gamble, and the Hong Kong Jockey Club is their only legal outlet. The **Hong Kong Racing Museum** (Tue–Sun 10am–5pm, until 9pm on race nights), in the Happy Valley Stand, tells the story in full and offers a superb view of the track, which can also be enjoyed through the huge glass windows of **Moon Koon** (see page 111).

The cemeteries

Across Wong Nai Chung Road are Hong Kong's oldest **cemeteries** (daily 8am–6pm). The **Parsi Cemetery** is the most picturesque, with its lush greenery. Older headstones in the **Colonial Cemetery** tell of early settlers' often-youthful deaths, while Portuguese memorials in **St Michael's Catholic Cemetery** highlight links with Macau. **Muslim** and **Jewish** cemeteries reflect other aspects of the colony's mix. When you're ready, catch a tram back to Wan Chai or Causeway Bay, or a bus south to Stanley or Aberdeen.

Food and Drink

❶ ZUSHI ANA
12/F Times Square, 1 Matheson Street, Causeway Bay; tel: 2526 1232; $$–$$$
Cool Japanese restaurant, specialising in sushi, with plenty of creative presentation. Hot dishes also served. Cocktails and Japanese beer and sake all available.

❷ HEICHINROU
11/F Times Square, 1 Matheson Street, Causeway Bay; tel: 2506 1212; $$$

Quality Chinese – mostly Cantonese – fare here and no MSG. Comfortable surroundings and good service make for a relaxed above-average meal.

❸ CITY'SUPER COOKED DELI
Basement Food Court, Times Square, 1 Matheson Street, Causeway Bay; www.citysuper.com.hk; $–$$
Top-quality fast-food counters that cater to every taste – Indian, Korean, Cantonese, French patisserie, hot dogs and international desserts.

Resting in Hollywood Road Park

HOLLYWOOD ROAD

A walk along Hollywood Road from its Sheung Wan origins to its newer role as the entry point to fashionable SoHo, encompassing temples, a backstreet flea market and a huge choice of antiques shops and art galleries.

DISTANCE: 2km (1.25 miles)
TIME: 2 to 3 hours
START: Hollywood Road Park
END: Pottinger Street, SoHo
POINTS TO NOTE: From The Landmark in Central, bus no. 10 to Kennedy Town stops at the Sheung Wan Civic Centre just before Possession Street, where the route starts.

HOLLYWOOD ROAD PARK

Hollywood Road is the centre of the art and antiques trade in Hong Kong, lined with shops selling all manner of things from the oriental past, from period furniture to Mao memorabilia. Start at **Possession Street** where the Royal Navy landed in 1841 to claim Hong Kong Island in the name of Queen Victoria.

Walk up the hill to Hollywood Road. On the left of the junction is the Hollywood Centre, a small arcade packed with ceramics and furniture shops. Turn right, and cross the street, where, next to new restaurants, serviced apartments and modern galleries, you still find traditional coffin makers. **Hollywood Road Park ❶**, with its Chinese gateway, still provides the living with a pleasant spot to while away free time.

Paak Sing Hall

Cross to the south side of Hollywood Road, where trendy Po Yan Street leads to **Tai Ping Shan Street**. Here, the legendary pirate Cheung Po Tsai settled after receiving amnesty from the Qing emperor, some 30 years before the British arrived. Just to the right is **Paak Sing** ('100 Names') **Ancestral Hall ❷**, founded in 1856 to house the ancestor tablets that Hong Kong's settlers brought with them from the mainland. There are several thousand wooden tablets inside, and a variety of shrines.

Temple of Mercy

Follow Tai Ping Shan Street east; a shrine on the left and a vividly coloured temple further on are both dedicated to **Kwun Yam ❸** (or Guanyin), Goddess of Mercy. Turn left down Sai Street to get back to Hollywood Road.

Incense at Man Mo Temple

Shopping at Cat Street market

CAT STREET

Make a detour left down **Ladder Street** – made up of broad stone steps – then turn left again into **Upper Lascar Row**, home to the bustling 'Cat Street' ④ flea market. No one agrees on the origin of this name. Some say cat burglars and pirates fenced their spoils here; others that street peddlers are known as 'cats' and their wares as 'mouse goods' in Chinese; still others claim that it's a reference to prostitutes. All are plausible,

as this was once the heart of a crowded slum, notorious for opium dens, gambling parlours and brothels. What is certain is that people have been trading antiques and second-hand goods here for 150 years; now, amid curio stalls is the **Man Mo Café**, see ①.

Back on Hollywood Road is one of the island's oldest temples, the **Man Mo** ⑤ (c.1842), dedicated to the Gods of Literature and War (and the protector of antiques dealers). Just around the corner is **The Press Room** (see page 109).

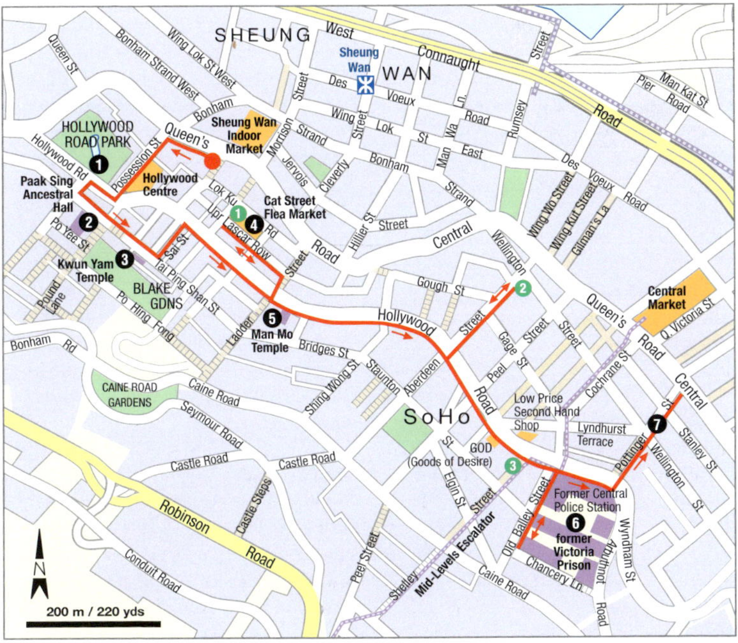

Lin Heung Tea House

MOVING UPMARKET

Continuing east along Hollywood Road pass dozens of antiques shops. When it's time for refreshments to review your finds, there are plenty of options in **SoHo** (from **So**uth of **Ho**llywood Road, though it now extends either side). A detour left down Aberdeen Street will lead to a kind of monument, the **Lin Heung**, see ②.

You can also rummage for relics and old photos of Hong Kong at the **Low Price Second Hand Shop**, an open-fronted bric-a-brac shop on the corner of Lyndhurst Terrace, or find an ironic take on Hong Kong culture at **G.O.D.** (Goods of Desire), across the road. The Mid-Levels Escalator crosses Hollywood Road here and heads up Shelley Street. **Motorino**, see ③, is a good pitstop.

Art galleries and antiques shops give way to boutiques and restaurants on the remaining part of Hollywood Road. The imposing buildings across the street are the former **Central Police Station and Victoria Prison** ⑥. The earliest of these monuments to colonial law and order were built in 1864.

Wyndham and Pottinger streets
Beyond the police station Hollywood Road becomes **Wyndham Street** (see page 45) at the top of **Pottinger Street** ⑦. Named after the first governor of Hong Kong, the latter's Chinese name is far simpler – stone step street. Head east along Wyndham Street, Hong Kong's newest cocktail bar zone, or walk down Pottinger Street back to Queen's Road.

Food and Drink

❶ MAN MO CAFÉ
40 Upper Lascar Row, Sheung Wan, tel; 2644 5644; $$
Enjoy well-rendered dumplings, Chinese-style filled buns and soup, rice and noodles with twists, prepared by chefs with top French and Chinese restaurant backgrounds. There is a small terrace overlooking Cat Street bazaar.

❷ LIN HEUNG TEA HOUSE
160–4 Wellington Street, Central; tel: 2544 2556; closed 4.30–5.30pm; $

If you want an authentic *yum cha* experience, this is it: busy, with relentless noise, minimal English menu listings and communal round tables. Fresh dim sum is served 6am–3.30pm – just stop passing trolleys, open the bamboo steamers and point to what you want. Dinner is Cantonese comfort food.

❸ MOTORINO
14 Shelley Street, SoHo, Central; tel: 2801 6881; $$
A slice of New York – well, New York pizzas to be precise. Launched in 2013, this popular open-fronted joint is a good pitstop.

On the Mid-Levels Escalator

LAN KWAI FONG, WYNDHAM STREET AND SOHO

The high concentration of bars and restaurants in this area of Hong Kong Island's Central District – where Hong Kong plays hard – makes it easy to wander around and find a venue to suit your mood.

DISTANCE: Varies (see Points to Note)
TIME: An evening
START: Central MTR, Exit D2
END: Staunton and Elgin streets
POINTS TO NOTE: Since this is an evening stroll, with plenty of places to stop off to have a drink, a meal or just look around, the precise route is a personal choice, and the time and distance involved are entirely notional.

Nightlife in Central clusters around the narrow streets and lanes in between the main business district and the Mid-Levels residential area. The two main areas, **Lan Kwai Fong** and **SoHo**, are just a short walk apart, and **Wyndham Street**, which connects the two, offers even more bars, restaurants and clubs.

Lan Kwai Fong is a small area that claims more restaurants and after-dark entertainment per block than anywhere else in Hong Kong. Once for expats-only, today LKF has a clientele that's a snapshot of the international mix working and living in Hong Kong. English is spoken here, with many accents. It can all be slightly tacky, however, so if you prefer a more down-to-earth vibe, SoHo establishments should appeal. SoHo is also home to quirky boutiques and shops selling homeware and vintage items; many of these are run by young designers, and some sell one-off pieces.

LAN KWAI FONG

Start your night with a stroll around Lan Kwai Fong. Walk up D'Aguilar Street from Central MTR, via the signposted exit (D2). **Lan Kwai Fong ❶** itself is a short L-shaped lane that intersects the bending **D'Aguilar Street** at either end, forming a kind of square.

One of Lan Kwai Fong's veteran establishments (**Post 97**), morphed in 2012 into the Italian-flavoured Il Posto 97, see ❶, and is a relaxing place to meet for dinner, drinks or a coffee; **Club 97** downstairs is a bit wilder, with a range of music nights.

Head up to the top of the street, where the open-sided **Marlin** (56 D'Aguilar

Central nightlife

Street) Martini bar on the corner gamely is laid back, or bear right for lively **Stormies** bar (46–50 D'Aguilar Street). Across the road in Lan Kwai Fong tower is Hard Rock Café **Hong Kong**.

Dining out

When hunger pangs strike, most of the bars can serve snacks and often something larger, too. On D'Aguilar Street ❷ more international food options include **Al's Diner**'s legendary burgers,

and Mexican snacks and 150 different kinds of tequila at **Agave**.

Just across the junction from the very top of D'Aguilar Street, the **Fringe Club** (see page 29 and page 118) is worth investigating, whether for performances, to chill on the roof-garden, or to enjoy an exhibition in the main bar. For late-night music, back at 38–44 D'Aguilar, **Insomnia** has house bands playing covers, while in the basement the much more hip **Volar**

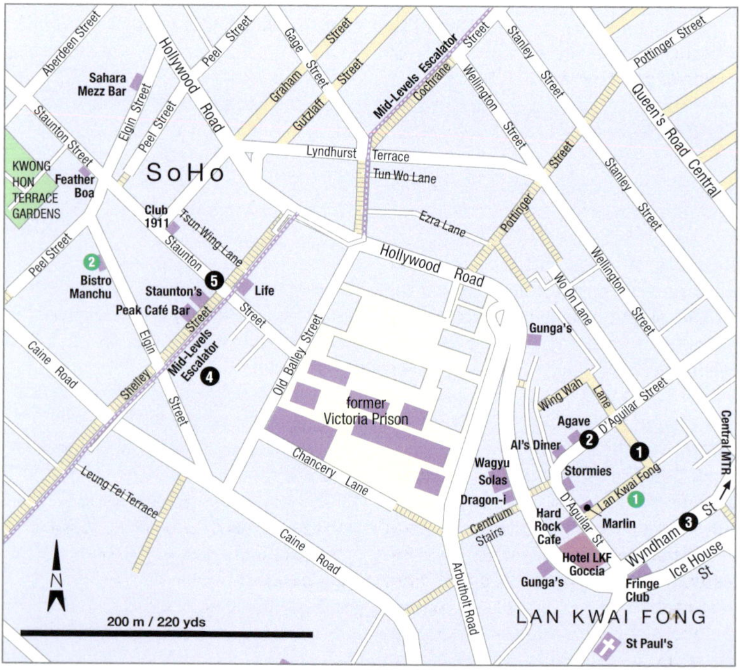

hosts some of Hong Kong's best, most varied DJ sessions,

WYNDHAM STREET

On the way from Lan Kwai Fong to SoHo, there's a string of upscale yet relaxed venues to visit. **Wyndham Street** ❸ is home to great international-style bar-restaurants such as **Goccia** (see page 107) and has a boutique hotel (Hotel LKF; LKF Tower, no. 33). In the same building, you can tuck into Portuguese cuisine and wine at at **Casa Lisboa**, or for retro prohibition chic enjoy cocktails and food at Lily & Bloom.

A few doors down at no. 57, **Gunga's** has been serving excellent Indian fare for over 20 years. Across the road at the Centrium building (no. 60), **Wagyu** offers a steak-heavy menu and is open to the street for relaxed dining and after-work drinks. **Dragon-i** (see page 120) is long a destination of choice for the beautiful crowd; **Solas**, downstairs, is a more intimate music-focused venue.

SOHO

Of all the Central nightlife areas, SoHo has the most atmosphere, though it only developed as a nightlife zone after the **Mid-Levels Escalator** ❹ was completed in 1994. It spreads out from **Staunton Street** ❺, **Elgin Street**, and the streets around the Mid-Levels Escalator.

Good SoHo drinking haunts include **Staunton's** Wine Bar + Café (10 Staunton Street), the *fin-de-siècle* drawing-room **Feather Boa** (no. 38) and **Club 1911** (no. 27), with a feel of old Shanghai. For dinner, take your pick of Moroccan delicacies at **Sahara Mezz Bar** (11 Elgin Street), Manchurian dishes at **Bistro Manchu**, see ❷, also on Elgin Street, the lively **Peak Café Bar** (no. 9–13) and vegetarian **Life** (no. 10; see page 108), both situated beside the escalator on Shelley Street, or dozens of other global cuisines on offer in the area.

Food and Drink

❶ IL POST 97

U/G 9 Lan Kwai Fong, Central; tel: 2186 1816; $–$$$
This casual, relaxed venue is a spruced up now Italian reworking of an old international favourite. Its menu is reasonably priced for the reliable quality, and, when you feel like, it it's an easy transfer to Club 97 downstairs.

❷ BISTRO MANCHU

33 Elgin Street, SoHo, Central; tel: 2536 9218; $$
Authentic northern Chinese cooking is served at this cosy, colourful restaurant. There are lots of intriguing-sounding Manchurian dishes both with and without chilli, plus some highly recommended lamb and delicious dumplings.

Blue House on Stone Nullah Lane

WAN CHAI AFTERNOON

Explore the backstreets, markets and temples of old Wan Chai, then head for the harbour and the spectacular new waterfront, a gleaming symbol of post-colonial Hong Kong built on reclaimed land.

DISTANCE: 3.5km (2.25 miles)
TIME: 2–3 hours
START: Wan Chai MTR
END: Wan Chai Ferry Pier
POINTS TO NOTE: This route divides into two parts: old Wan Chai and the commercial area and giant arts and exhibition venues north of Gloucester Road. Exploring this area means walking along many pedestrian bridges and walkways: figuring them out is a distinctive Hong Kong experience.

OLD WAN CHAI

From Wan Chai MTR (Exit A3, on O'Brien Road), cross over the Johnston Road tramlines, and then proceed down **Tai Yuen Street ❶**, which, together with some of the neighbouring side streets, still retains much of the flavour of old Hong Kong. Walk east through the bustling street markets of **Cross Street** and **Wan Chai Road**, then cross Queen's Road East, and walk up **Stone Nullah Lane**, looking out for the **Blue House** at

no. 72 (closed to visitors), a 1920s tenement building with wooden staircases and metal balconies. On the same road is Stone Nullah Tavern (no. 69), an upscale American bar serving, among other things, US craft beers and home-made sausages and pickles. Almost at the end of the lane, shaded by trees, is the **Pak Tai Temple ❷** (1860s), which contains a 3m (10ft) copper statue of the Daoist god Pak Tai that is said to be over 400 years old.

The first waterfront

Retrace your steps to **Queen's Road East**, which marks Wan Chai's original waterfront. It is now best known for soft furnishings stores and shops selling traditional rattan and rosewood furniture. Head west as far as the former **Wan Chai Post Office ❸** (1912), on the corner of Wan Chai Gap Road. This quaint whitewashed building served as the district's post office until 1992; nowadays it houses the **Environmental Resource Centre** (Wed–Mon 10am–5pm). Take a look inside at the original wooden counter and red post-boxes.

TOWERS AND TEMPLES

Now head west to the circular 66-storey **Hopewell Centre** ❹, the tallest building in town in the 1980s, and ride the glass-bubble lift for some of the city's most spectacular views. In its shadow, to the west, is the **Hung Shing (Tai Wong) Temple** ❺, from 1860. You can smell the incense before you see it. As befits its former waterfront location, the temple is dedicated to one of the patron gods of fishermen. Notice the boulders incorporated into its design, and the sacred banyan tree behind it.

Tai Wong Street

Cross back over Queen's Road East and walk down **Tai Wong Street East** ❻, a characteristically eclectic Wan Chai street, with tea shops and a clutch of restaurants, including the popular **International Curry House** and a meditation centre that also hosts the **World Peace Café**, see ❶ and ❷. At no. 20 is the old **Woo Cheong Pawn Shop**, with distinctive tall counters inside – and a gaudy neon sign points it out after sundown.

Note that round the corner, Johnston Road is a good place to stop for some bargain hunting at the jostling factory outlets. At no. 62, are three century-old shophouses, which have been beautifully restored and converted into **The Pawn** restaurant (see page 111).

Continue the route, though, along Luard Road, which runs north from the junction of Tai Wong Street and Johnston Road. This street is the heart of Wan Chai's nightlife district, covered in full in the next route (see page 50).

Johnston Road and Queen's Road East are at the heart of an urban-renewal programme, which has sparked interest in Wan Chai's heritage. A number of old-style streets, such as Lee Tung Street, once home to specialist printing shops, no longer exist; other streets, including Tai Yuen Street, mentioned, have been saved. Tai Wong Street and most of Cross Street market are likely to remain, surrounded by shiny new skyscrapers.

RECLAMATION

When you reach the multi-lane Gloucester Road, take any pedestrian bridge across, towards the imposing government departmental towers of the Inland Revenue and Immigration. These skyscrapers built on reclaimed land form the 'new' Wan Chai, a concentration of huge buildings linked by a web of pedestrian bridges.

To the left is the **Hong Kong Academy for Performing Arts (APA)** ❼ (see page 118), a college of dance, music and drama that doubles as a performance venue. To the right in Harbour Road is the **Hong Kong Arts Centre** ❽, dedicated to contemporary art and culture, with galleries, a theatre, a cinema, a shop and the **Pumpernickel Café**, see ❸.

Central's skyline as seen from inside the HKCEC

The Convention Centre

Leave the Arts Centre by the footbridge on the second floor, and cross over Harbour Road. The first stairway to the right leads down through a small sculpture garden and enters the impressive lobby of the **Grand Hyatt, Hong Kong** hotel. The stairs on the right lead into the **Hong Kong Convention and Exhibition Centre (HKCEC)** ❾. This building first opened in 1988, but an extension on a reclaimed semi-'island' built into the harbour more than doubled its size; the extension was completed in 1997, just in time for it to serve as the venue for the historic Handover Ceremony on 30 June, when China resumed sovereignty over Hong Kong. Such is the demand for exhibition space in Hong Kong that a second expansion was completed in 2009. Take the escalator into the new building, and walk through its many corridors and open spaces towards the harbour.

The Golden Bauhinia

Leave the complex at the Expo Drive entrance, and walk along **Expo Prom-**

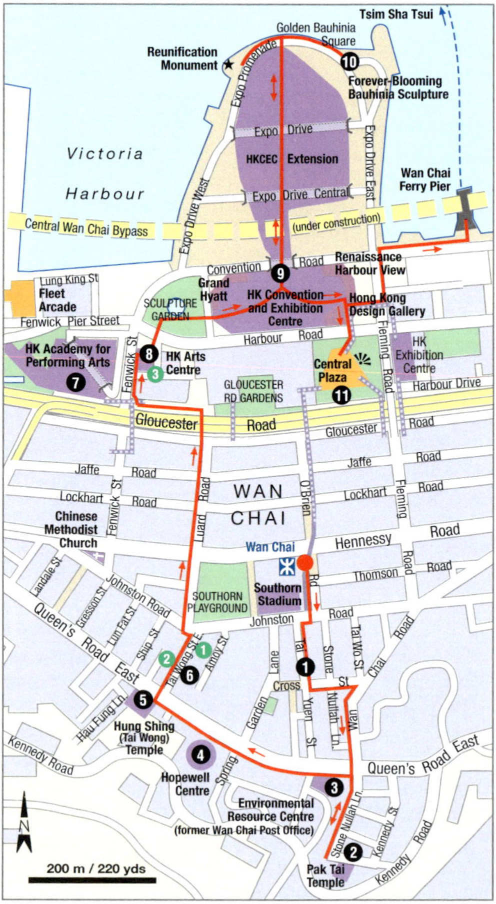

Fishing with a view

enade for dramatic views of the Harbour and Kowloon. This is a favourite photo-opportunity spot for mainland Chinese tourists, who like to pose by the black **Reunification Monument**, commemorating the 1997 handover, and by the golden **Forever-Blooming Bauhinia** ❿ sculpture. The elegant orchid-like bauhinia is an indigenous flower and Hong Kong's emblem; its five petals appear on the territory's red-and-white flag and on coins.

If you want to linger for a while longer in this area, you can eat well and enjoy fabulous views from the floor-to-ceiling windows at the centre's **Congress restaurant**, (see page 111).

CENTRAL PLAZA

Retrace your steps to the HKCEC's main entrance and follow signs to the **Renaissance Harbour View** mall, where the **Hong Kong Design Gallery** (Mon–Sun 10am–7.30pm) showcases original Hong Kong design.

Continue out through the mall and follow signs for **Central Plaza** ⓫, which rises 78 floors to 374m (1,227ft). The Sky Lobby on the 46th floor acts a free viewing gallery (Mon–Fri 8am–8pm, Sat 8am–2pm), as well as a changeover spot for lifts for some of the 6,000 people who work here. Sky City Church on its 75th floor is the world's highest church set in a skyscraper.

After returning to earth, follow signs back to Wan Chai MTR station or take the Star Ferry to Tsim Sha Tsui from the nearby Wan Chai Ferry Pier. Alternatively, explore Wan Chai after dark (see page 50).

Food and Drink

❶ INTERNATIONAL CURRY HOUSE

G/F 26–39 Tai Wong Street East, Wan Chai; tel: 2529 0088; $$
This small neighbourhood café has been serving up curries from across South and East Asia for three decades. Food is as spicy as you like, from mild Malaysian satays and coconut-rich laksa to vindaloos.

❷ WORLD PEACE CAFÉ

21–23 Tai Wong Street East, Wan Chai; tel: 2527 5870; $
This organic and vegetarian café run by a Buddhist organisation doubles as a meditation centre and is largely staffed by volunteers. Stop by for healthy lunch sets, juices and lassis.

❸ PUMPERNICKEL CAFÉ

4/F Hong Kong Arts Centre, 2 Harbour Road, Wan Chai; tel: 2588 1001; $
This is an ideal place to research arts events while taking in the view. Homemade breads, pastries and sandwiches plus great coffee and some substantial lunch set menus add to the appeal.

Traffic on Lockhart Road

WAN CHAI AFTER DARK

Buzzing after-work bars, clubs, cinemas, music and arts venues and restaurants of all sorts rub shoulders with the remaining girlie-bars of Suzie Wong fame. Mix your own Wan Chai cocktail, and join one of the best parties in town.

DISTANCE: Varies
TIME: All night
START: Wan Chai MTR
END: Star Street
POINTS TO NOTE: This route can be easily segmented, if you don't fancy doing all of it. Everywhere in Wan Chai is accessible by tram, bus or MTR, and ferries run to Tsim Sha Tsui from near the Convention Centre. If you plan on making a whole night of it, taxis are plentiful here too.

Nearly six decades on, Wan Chai is still inveterately linked with Richard Mason's 1957 risqué novel *The World of Suzie Wong*, and the 1960 film version starring William Holden and Nancy Kwan. Today, it offers a far more eclectic mix of night-time entertainment than it did in its heyday as a raunchy retreat for US servicemen during the Korean and Vietnam wars. Hostess bars have been eclipsed by trendy ones, and there is an increasingly thriving restaurant scene.

ARTS AND MUSIC

The remorseless **Wan Chai Reclamation**, snatching land away from Victoria Harbour, has provided land for hotels, malls, offices and dazzling arts and exhibition venues in an area sometimes referred to as North Wan Chai. Along with City Hall in Central and the Cultural Centre on the Tsim Sha Tsui waterfront, this is one of Hong Kong's foremost areas for live performances of all kinds. Even today's waterfront is temporary, as the final phase, with a major new highway bypass and rail link, is due to be completed by 2020.

If you're a fan of contemporary art, theatre or a film buff, begin by leaving Wan Chai MTR at Exit C and walking down Luard Road to see what's on at the harbourfront **Hong Kong Arts Centre** ❶ (www.hkac.org.hk). Just nearby, the **Hong Kong Academy of Performing Arts** ❷ (www.hkapa.edu) hosts local and visiting theatre companies, concerts by both its own students and an increasing roster of international acts, including productions of Austral-

Wan Chai at night   *Live music at Dusk Till Dawn*

ian, Broadway and West End musicals. Biggest of all, the **Hong Kong Convention and Exhibition Centre (HKCEC)** ❸ (www.hkcec.com) is a frequent venue for big-name international rock and pop acts.

Eating and drinking
Wan Chai's waterfront has a few elegant options for dining and socialising hidden away. The **Grand Hyatt** hotel, on one side of the Convention Centre, has two of Hong Kong's most acclaimed restaurants: **Grissini** (top-notch Italian) and **One Harbour Road** (refined Cantonese), both combining sensational harbour views and glamour. The Grand Hyatt's **Champagne Bar** is also one of the most classily opulent drinking spots in town. The HKCEC has a number of eating and drinking spots too – Golden Bauhinia, like a few others, is open whether exhibitions are on or not, and offers elevated Cantonese fare and service.

For a more low-key (and cheaper) evening, you could combine a show with a meal at **Jack's Terraza**, see

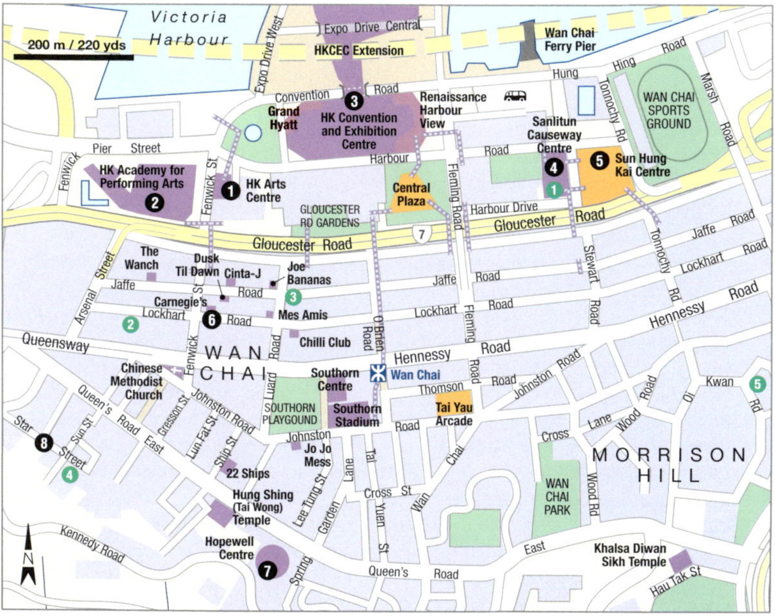

Mixing a drink at Carnegie's

, or anywhere in the nearby **Sanlitun Causeway Centre** . Sanlitun is ideal for couples and mixed groups to dine, off the main drag with a lively, mainly local, after-work crowd. The Lockhart Road area is where people really let their hair down – more of a raucous stag- and hen-night (batchelor/batcherlorette party) vibe. Star Street is a cool, chic hang-out with prices to match.

The building next door, the **Sun Hung Kai Centre**  offers a choice of sophisticated restaurants with great harbour views, including **Tamarind** (see page 112), which also hosts comedy acts.

GLOBAL CHOICES

To make a night of it after eating, you don't need to look far either. From the Convention Centre area, find your way through the pedestrian bridges over Gloucester Road, and head up Luard Road. There is an apparently endless choice of places to eat: local institutions such as the (North Chinese) **American Restaurant**, see , colonial-style-Indian **Jo Jo Mess** at 86–90 Johnston Road, or Chili Club (88 Lockhart Road), which has a loyal following for its Thai cuisine.

Cinta-J (69 Jaffe Road) has enjoyable Filipino-Indonesian-Malaysian food, then becomes a cocktail lounge, often with live music, as the night runs on. Of Wan Chai's drinking spots, **Delaney's**, see , is a reliable landmark.

WONG'S WORLD

The boisterous, nonstop hub of Wan Chai nightlife is still in the same place that it was in the Suzie Wong era, although today you can no longer step out from here straight onto the waterfront, as you could in the 1950s. It's centred on **Lockhart Road**  and **Jaffe Road**, above all where they cross **Luard Road** and **Fenwick Street**. There are no longer many sailors around, nor that many black-curtained girlie bars with morose doormen. There are some with beckoning hostesses outside, but it's a tame scene. Compared to the more sharp-and-stylish parts of Hong Kong, the atmosphere is laid-back and unfussy, with prices that are fairly pain-free.

MUSIC AND DANCING

If you want to hear some live music, check out tiny, down-to-earth **The Wanch** (54 Jaffe Road) or **Carnegie's** (53–5 Lockhart Road), an American bar with excellent music and a party vibe. **Mes Amis** on a key Wan Chai corner at 83 Lockhart Road is a great people-watching spot that changes from pub and wine bar in the early evening to wild dance bar late-night. **Joe Bananas** (23 Luard Road) is one of Wan Chai's most fun, full-on, old-fashioned discos. And for carrying on until sunrise, try **Dusk Till Dawn** (76 Jaffe Road) with its cover bands – this is an option that will carry on until after 7am.

Wan Chai taxi stand

STAR STREET

Finding the more upmarket nightlife scene in Wan Chai means heading for the older part of the district, located to the south of Johnston Road. There are plenty more restaurants: you can spin while you dine on edgy Spanish cuisine at revolving restaurant View 62 by Paco Roncero (62/F **Hopewell Centre**) ❼, reached by a swish glass-bubble lift.

To discover the most fashionable spot hereabouts, though, head west along Queen's Road East to Wing Fung Street, then turn left up it to **Star Street** ❽, a short lane that is one of Hong Kong's newer style enclaves. There are shops, cafés and, above all, bar-restaurants such as **1/5 Nuevo**, see ❹.

Not far from Star Street, are two well-thought-of standalone Spanish restaurants worth seeking out, such as 22 Ships (22 Ship Street), with its modern tapas menu, and **Catalunya**, see ❺.

Food and Drink

❶ JACK'S TERRAZA
Shop 8, 1/F Sanlitun Causeway Centre, 28 Harbour Road, Wan Chai; tel: 2827 1687; $$
Sample the ambience of bustling Sanlitun's dozen or more restaurants by dining alfresco on the terrace. The food here is pasta, pizza, steaks and seafood.

❷ AMERICAN RESTAURANT
G/F 20 Lockhart Road, Wan Chai; tel: 2527 7277; $$
Don't let the name fool you: the 'American' has been serving tasty Northern Chinese food (great Peking duck) for over 50 years.

❸ DELANEY'S
G-1/F One Capital Place, 18 Luard Road, Wan Chai; tel: 2804 2880; $$
Always-buzzing Irish pub and sports bar with football, rugby and more sports on a big screen upstairs, and a quieter bar below. Guinness on tap and excellent, hearty food.

❹ 1/5 NUEVO
Starcrest Building, 9 Star Street, Wan Chai; tel: 2529 2300; $$
'One-Fifth Nuevo' is the hub of the new smarter Wan Chai scene. It's a two-storey, very hip, high-ceilinged bar, with casual dining and Spanish-inspired food. The bar eases effortlessly into an ever-so-cool club as the night goes on.

❺ CATALUNYA
Guardian House, 32 Oi Kwan Road, Wan Chai; tel: 2866 7900; $$$
This restaurant has a popular lounge-bar overlooking a quiet, leafy street as well as a spacious, more formal dining area. As is clear from the name, the cuisine is Catalan, combining Spanish, French and Middle Eastern influences. Great cocktails, too.

Waiting for the tram

VICTORIA PEAK

One of the world's steepest funicular railways, the spectacular Peak Tram has been running up Victoria Peak since 1888, and is one of Hong Kong's must–do rides. The climb takes 8 minutes. From the top, enjoy a full view of the architectural forest below and take time out to explore the city's green mountain.

DISTANCE: 4km (2.5 miles)
TIME: Half to a full day
START/END: Peak Tram Lower Terminus, Garden Road, Central
POINTS TO NOTE: To reach the start point, walk from Admiralty MTR through Hong Kong Park (about 10 mins) or take bus 15C from the Central Ferry Piers via Connaught Road.

Food and Drink

❶ BUBBA GUMP SHRIMP CO

Level 3, Peak Tower; tel: 2849 2867; $$
American restaurant serving huge portions of shrimp, Southern-style dishes and Forrest Gump's favourite puds.

❷ CAFÉ DECO BAR & GRILL

Level 1–2, Peak Galleria, 118 Peak Road; tel: 2849 5111; $$$
An eclectic fusion menu with seafood, steaks and Italian and Thai influences.

The **Peak Tram** ❶ (7am–midnight; approx. every 15 mins) runs up to the base of the 373m (1,223ft) **Peak Tower** ❷. Designed in 1997 by British architect Terry Farrell in the shape of an upheld rice bowl, the seven-storey complex is topped by the **Sky Terrace** 428 (Mon–Fri 10am–11pm, Sat, Sun and public hols 8am–11pm; charge), from where there are stunning views.

Attractions inside the tower include **Madame Tussaud's** waxworks museum plus plenty of places to eat and admire the view, including the **Pearl on the Peak** (see page 109) and **Bubba Gump Shrimp Co**, see ❶.

Across the road from the Tower is the **Peak Galleria** ❸, less architecturally spectacular but with four floors of shops and restaurants, and a viewing platform. Also nearby is one of the most relaxing places to take in the view, the **Peak Lookout** (see page 29).

AROUND THE PEAK

Walk south from the Peak Tower into **Lugard Road**, the start of a gentle cir-

On the Peak Trail

A rewarding view from the Peak

cular walk around Victoria Peak, which takes about an hour to complete. The tree-lined path winds past isolated colonial villas that are among the most expensive and exclusive homes in the territory, far removed from the metropolis below. On clear days (sadly, increasingly rare) you can see beyond the harbour and Kowloon to the Nine Dragon Ridge, which separates urban Hong Kong from the New Territories, and across to the hills up to Shenzhen.

Lugard Road merges with **Harlech Road** ❹ at a four-path junction and shaded picnic spot. The path winds east along the wooded southern flank of the mountain back to the Peak Tower.

Up to the top

If you're feeling energetic, continue on up **Mt Austin Road**, which after a 20-minute climb runs out at the summit of **Victoria Peak** ❺, at 552m (1,811ft). On the way, make a detour into **Victoria Peak Gardens** ❻, for more views. A path, the **Governor's Walk**, runs around the gardens –all that remains of the early governors' summer residence.

It is possible to walk back to Central from the Peak Tower –follow the marked paths downhill (allow 45 mins). Alternatively, back by the tram station, grab a drink at **Café Deco**, see ❷, which offers great views, before catching a tram back downhill.

Jumbo Kingdom

SOUTHSIDE

*Hong Kong Island's alter ego: a leisurely exploration of the still–uncrowded
south shore, with the floating restaurants of Aberdeen, family fun at Ocean Park,
beaches in Repulse Bay, and the seaside market town of Stanley.*

DISTANCE: 10km (6 miles)
TIME: At least half a day, excluding
Ocean Park
START: Aberdeen
END: Stanley
POINTS TO NOTE: For Aberdeen, take
7 or 71 bus from the Central Ferry
Piers bus station; from Aberdeen, then
take bus 48 from Aberdeen Main Road
to get to Ocean Park, or bus 73 to
Repulse Bay and Stanley. Weekends
and holidays are very busy, especially at
Ocean Park and Stanley.

Within a short distance of Central, Hong
Kong Island's south side offers respite from the intensely urbanised north
shore. To the surprise of many visitors,
much of it still consists of forested
mountains, sweeping vistas, small
towns and villages and broad bays with
fine beaches. The four main attractions – Aberdeen Harbour, Ocean Park,
Repulse Bay and Stanley – are all easily
accessible by bus. The journey is part of
the fun, as there are some breathtaking
views along the way as the road winds
over mountains and around the coast.

ABERDEEN

Buses arrive at **Aberdeen Bus Station**.
From here, take either the footbridge or
subway across Aberdeen Praya Road to
Hong Kong's liveliest waterfront. The
promenade has been enhanced with
trees, benches and signs with potted
histories of different sights.

The harbour
Aberdeen ❶ itself is still very much
a working harbour. The attractive
sight of a harbour full of fishing boats
belies the fact, though, that Hong Kong
waters' fish stocks are critically low
after decades of overfishing. This has
been a fishing port for hundreds of
years, long before the British decided
to name it after their Foreign Secre-
tary, Lord Aberdeen, in the 1840s. Its
Chinese name, *Heung Kong Tsai* (Little
Fragrant Harbour), is thought to allude
to the port's centuries-old trade in fragrant incense wood.

Ocean Park ride   *Shek O beach*

Sampans and floating restaurants

A sampan ride through this crowded waterway is a highlight of any visit. The sampan operators (often elderly women) are always ready to negotiate a fee for an occasionally hair-raising spin between the fishing trawlers, ramshackle live-aboard junks, and pleasure craft.

Another way to take a trip through the harbour is on the free shuttle boats (signposted at points along Aberdeen waterfront) to the magnificently gaudy **Jumbo Kingdom**, see ❶, Aberdeen's famous 'floating restaurants', celebrated in films set in Hong Kong for over 50 years. The huge multi-deck illuminated pagodas have had a makeover recently, but the over-the-top gold dragons and the grand entrance remain the same. The Dragon Court and Jumbo Chinese restaurants are on the first and second floors, and the rooftop has been transformed into the **Top Deck**, see ❷, a bar and restaurant that is a destination in itself.

From Aberdeen you can take a shopping detour at nearby Ap Lei Chau –

home to Horizon Plaza, which is full of warehouse-size stores selling furniture, home furnishings and end-of-season designer clothes.

OCEAN PARK

Ocean Park ❷ (www.oceanpark.com.hk; daily 10am–6.30pm; charge), on the peninsula east of Aberdeen, is Hong Kong's longest-running theme park and oceanarium. Despite competition from Disneyland (see page 74), it is still a local favourite, drawing over five million visitors a year, with plenty of new rides and animal attractions launched since 2010 and onsite hotels under development. The oceanariums and spectacular cliff-top setting make it enjoyable even if theme parks usually leave you cold. Buses run direct to the park from various parts of Hong Kong.

Marine life, rides and pandas

Highlights of Ocean Park include the stunning Aqua City, with the Grand Aquarium at its centre – a mesmerising walk-through descending four-storeys underwater and featuring rays and sharks among others – and habitats for both two kinds of Chinese panda (the famous giant black-and-white variety and the lesser-seen red panda, also from China). Seals and sea lions, as well as dolphins can also be seen – including in regular aquatic shows. There are also thrills of increasing degrees, from escalator rides up and down the headland and the Abyss Turbo Drop. Allow at least four hours to explore, especially if visiting with children.

REPULSE BAY

Beyond the Ocean Park headland there open up two of the most beautiful stretches of coastline on the island, **Deep Water Bay** and **Repulse Bay ❸**. The most common theory for the latter's name is that the bay was once used as a refuge by pirates, who were

---

Tai Tam Country Park

A huge amount of Hong Kong Island, especially towards the south side, is given over to country parks; the largest is the Tai Tam, which covers most of the mountain ridge between Causeway Bay and Stanley. To explore it, take a no. 6, 61 or 66 bus from Exchange Square in Central to Parkview on Wong Nai Chung Gap Road, from where it's a fairly undemanding, downhill hike past glittering reservoirs to Tai Tam Road (about 2km/1.25 miles). From this point you can get buses back to town or to Stanley, or try a tougher walk over the 'Dragon's Back' to the laid-back village of Shek O (16km/10 miles). Alternatively, do the 'Wilson Trail' down from Wong Nai Chung Gap to Stanley (5km/3 miles), taking in some superb views.

Ever-popular Ocean Park

'repulsed' by the British Navy in the 1840s. It's hard to find a spare centimetre of sand on summer weekends, but the beaches are often deserted on weekdays. To get here from Ocean Park, turn right out of the main entrance and walk up to Wong Chuk Hang Road to catch the no. 73 bus from Aberdeen.

Repulse Bay Complex

Repulse Bay became a popular relaxation spot for Hong Kong colonials in the 1920s, when the Repulse Bay Hotel was built, an architectural gem and the belle of colonial society. Over the years Noël Coward, George Bernard Shaw, Marlon Brando and many more famous visitors were all refreshed by the view from its famous terrace.

Sadly, most of the hotel was swept aside in 1982 to make room for the **Repulse Bay Complex ❹**, with restaurants, a fancy spa, shops and plush apartment blocks, which have helped the Bay become an even more popular residential area for the wealthy. One, bright blue block has a large hole in the middle, allegedly introduced by the architect for feng shui reasons – to allow the dragon that lives inside the mountain behind to get down to the sea. But nevertheless, within the complex is a new-build luxurious partial reconstruction of the original **Repulse Bay Hotel** incorporating parts of the old building, now a complex simply called The Repulse Bay. It has lovely

restaurant, The **Verandah**, see ❸, which effectively recalls the old days in décor and service. It enjoys the same celebrated view as its predecessor, and is one of Hong Kong's most enjoyable brunch venues.

There are more economical eating options elsewhere near the beach, such as Pizza Hut and Pacific Coffee – the latter serving sandwiches and salads, as well as a kiosk right on the edge of the beach.

At the south end of the beach is the rather bizarre **Life Guard Club**, which looks more like a temple than a restaurant with its colourful collection of images, including huge statues of the Buddhist goddess Kwun Yam and her Daoist counterpart Tin Hau, both protectors of fishermen.

STANLEY

From Repulse Bay, catch a no. 73 bus again, or any bus marked for Stanley. The road hugs the picturesque coastline of **Chung Hom Wan** (bay), looking westward to Lamma Island. Like Aberdeen, **Stanley ❺** was a thriving fishing village long before the British arrived. The local Hakka people named it *Chek Chue* or 'robbers' lair', because it was a haven for smugglers and pirates. Nowadays, it's a residential enclave of wealthy commuters, with a seaside-village feel. There is a wide choice of restaurants and bars, and a buzzing street market.

Shopping in Stanley Market

Around Stanley Market

Stanley Market (daily 10am–6pm) is a maze of stalls and little shops, just down the hill from the bus stop on Stanley Village Road. Apart from the colourful food and flower section, it caters largely to tourists and expats. Prices may not be low, but it's still a great place to browse for gifts and souvenirs. Good buys include embroidered linen, silk and linen clothes, sportswear, pictures, chops (see page 35) and craftwork.

Head along **Stanley Main Street** past a strip of bars, bistros and pubs, and you will find a tiny **Tai Wong Temple** built into a rock, just before **Stanley Plaza**, a modern mall. On the opposite side of the plaza is a **Tin Hau Temple** that looks somewhat modern and functional, although a temple has been here since the 18th century. It houses an ancient drum and bell, dated 1767, which belonged to the

legendary Qing-dynasty pirate Cheung Po-Tsai, and the rather tatty skin of Hong Kong's last wild tiger, shot in Stanley in 1942.

The temple was once on the shoreline, but nowadays the promenade is dominated by **Murray House** ❻. Dating from 1848, this neoclassical former British officers' mess stood in Central Hong Kong until 1982, when it was taken apart piece by piece to make way for the Bank of China tower. After almost 20 years in storage, Murray House was reassembled and opened in 2001.

Inside, there's a good selection of restaurants such as **Wildfire**, see ❹, where you can take a break under whirring ceiling fans or enjoy the view from the balconies.

The beach and military cemetery

Later, head back towards the market and then continue along Wong Ma Kok Road towards the secluded **St Stephen's Beach**, and the well-tended **Stanley Military Cemetery** (daily 10am–7pm), where colonial soldiers and World War II prisoners of war are buried.

Head back into town along Stanley Village Road, past the **former Stanley Police Station** (1859, no. 88), the territory's oldest police building, and now a supermarket. There are lots of good places for watching the sunset over Stanley Bay over drinks or dinner: as well as those in Murray House, try **The**

East to Shek O

Beyond Stanley, Tai Tam Road winds its way to join Shek O Road, eventually leading to the eponymous village, and one of Hong Kong Island's best beaches. Shek O itself, accessed more directly from Central on the 309 bus, is a small residential outpost with a few good restaurants. Just to the north, Big Wave Bay is – as the name suggests – the SAR's premier surfing centre.

Swimmers on Shek O beach

Boathouse, see ⑤, on Stanley Main Street, or, for something more Chinese, the beautiful **Shu Zhai**, see ⑥. Afterwards, take the escalator through Stanley Plaza to the main road for buses back to the city.

Food and Drink

① JUMBO RESTAURANT
Jumbo Kingdom, Sham Wan Pier Drive, Aberdeen; tel: 2553 9111; $$–$$$
This place trades on its reputation as a Hong Kong institution, rather than the excellent food it serves. Maybe just order a dish or two to sample the atmosphere. Large, loud, bright and kitsch.

② TOP DECK AT THE JUMBO
Jumbo Kingdom, Sham Wan Pier Drive, Aberdeen; tel: 2552 3331; $$$
The highlight of many a visit to Aberdeen is a long lunch or dinner at Top Deck, followed by drinks while lounging on the sofas outside on the deck, overlooking flashy yachts and humble sampans. The décor is elegant oriental, making this a classy cousin to the loud Jumbo downstairs. The food is international, with Chinese, Japanese, Asian and European dishes and fresh imported seafood. Book ahead for the weekend brunch buffet.

③ VERANDAH
109 Repulse Bay Road, Repulse Bay; tel: 2292 2822; $$$$
An atmospheric evocation of the colonial era, with ceiling fans, palms, acres of 1930s-style woodwork and a stunning sea view. The menu is classic European, and afternoon tea and Sunday brunch are specialities. Always book for weekends.

④ WILDFIRE
2/F Murray House, Stanley; tel: 2813 6161; $$
Offering an exceptional choice of pizzas plus steaks, salads and seafood platters, Wildfire is on the top floor of beautiful Murray House. It's amply spacious, with high ceilings, a balcony, a children's play area and fine views across the bay.

⑤ THE BOATHOUSE
86–88 Stanley Main Street, Stanley; tel: 2813 4467; $$
A nautically oriented gastropub on the Stanley waterfront: tuck into seafood, salads, sandwiches, pasta, great fish and chips and other international favourites. It extends over three storeys, with a roof garden providing the best seats in the house.

⑥ SHU ZHAI
80 Stanley Main Street, Stanley; tel: 2813 0123; closed Mon; $$
This contemporary take on a traditional-style tea house, tucked behind the Dymocks store, is a shady retreat from the crowds. Choose between dim sum or modern Chinese cuisine, both served all day.

TSIM SHA TSUI

Visit the Hong Kong Museum of Art and The Peninsula – one of the world's great historic hotels – then continue north to Kowloon's shopping Golden Mile, dropping in on Kowloon Park and the Hong Kong Science Museum.

DISTANCE: 5.5km (3.25 miles)
TIME: Half to a full day
START/END: Star Ferry Pier, TST
POINTS TO NOTE: Consider timing your TST outing to ensure you are in a vantage spot at 8pm to catch the Symphony of Lights, the world's largest permanent sound-and-light show, which lights up the skyline of Kowloon and Hong Kong every night.

This route will help you get your bearings around Tsim Sha Tsui (pronounced 'chim-sa-choi'), the bustling district at the tip of the Kowloon peninsula. TST, as locals often call it, is known for its museums, hotels, restaurants, entertainment and the beginning of the 'Golden Mile' along Nathan Road, Kowloon's glittering shopping strip.

AROUND THE STAR FERRY

Start from Hong Kong Tourist Board's Kowloon office (daily 8am–8pm) by the **Star Ferry concourse ❶**, where TST ferries from Hong Kong Island arrive. To your left is Harbour City, a vast complex of upscale shopping malls and the Ocean Terminal, where cruise ships berth. Just in front – should you already be hungry at this point – there's great dim sum at **Jade Garden**, see ❶.

Former Marine Police HQ

Just across Canton Road is a white stucco 19th-century building that was the Marine Police Headquarters until 1996. It has now been thoroughly restored and reopened as **Hullett House** (www.hulletthouse.com), a 10-suite boutique hotel, with five restaurants. Below Hullett House, the small hill that gave marine policemen their vantage point has been converted into a brand-new faux-Victorian mall called 1881 Heritage – home to a handful of very top-tier timepiece, jewellery and fashion brands.

Old Kowloon station clock tower

Head back to the harbour and the 45m (147ft)-tall brick-and-stone **clock tower** dating from 1915. This

The skyline at night

is all that remains of the grand Kowloon–Canton Railway (KCR) Terminus, demolished in 1978. From here you could once take a train all the way through Asia to Paris.

Take the staircase near the clock tower up to the elevated promenade and observation gallery. The waterfront here offers such magnificent vistas of Hong Kong Island that it's hard to figure out what inspired the architect to design a windowless façade for the **Hong Kong Cultural Centre** ❷ (www.hkcultural centre.gov.hk). But aesthetics aside,

Old Kowloon's clock tower

the building is Hong Kong's premier venue for classical Western and Chinese music, ballet and theatre and the base of the Hong Kong Philharmonic and Hong Kong Chinese orchestras.

Hong Kong Museum of Art

Walk through the Cultural Centre to the **Hong Kong Museum of Art** ❸ (Fri and Sun–Wed 10am–6pm, Sat 10am–8pm; charge except Wed). It has superb collections of Chinese antiquities, paintings and calligraphy, contemporary Hong Kong art, and, perhaps most fascinating for many, pictures of old Hong Kong, Canton and Macau (third floor).

Hong Kong Space Museum

The large white dome just beyond it is the **Hong Kong Space Museum** ❹ (Mon and Wed–Fri 1–9pm, Sat–Sun 10am–9pm; charge except Wed), with lots of interactive exhibits aimed to keep kids enthralled and a high-tech planetarium with an Omnimax film theatre. The museum itself is quite compact and takes no more than an hour to see.

ALONG THE WATERFRONT

Just to the east, the waterfront promenade turns into the **Avenue of the Stars** ❺, a 440m (480 yard) -long tribute to the Hong Kong movie industry, with the harbour providing a perfect backdrop. Acting and directing achievements are commemorated Hollywood-style with brass stars and handprints in the pavement, and there's a statue of Hong Kong's most famous film star, Bruce Lee, and souvenir shops with Hong Kong movie memorabilia. For a lingering look at the harbour view, the terrace at **Deck N Beer** – which despite its name also serves food and soft drinks, see ❷, makes a handy stop, or turn away from the harbour and walk through the New World Centre mall to Salisbury Road. The replacement East Tsim Sha Tsui KCR train station is right across the street. Overlooking the new transport link is **Blackhead Signal Tower** ❻ (daily 9–11am and 4–6pm). The tower was built in 1907 to house the time-ball by which ships in the harbour adjusted their chronometers. From here, turn westwards back through an underground mall to the Peninsula.

The Peninsula

The **Peninsula** ❼ (see page 103) is the *grande dame* of Hong Kong hotels, and was the only choice for visiting celebrities and heads of state for some time after it opened in 1928. Amenities include the spectacular restaurant-bar **Felix** (see page 113), plus the superb gourmet French restaurant Gaddi's. However, it is the beautifully restored Peninsula Lobby that wins most visitors' hearts – a wonderfully atmospheric place to stop for coffee or a full afternoon tea (daily 2–7pm). In recognition of its popularity and social trends,

Hong Kong Cultural Centre

On the Avenue of the Stars

the dress code is a little more relaxed before 6.30pm.

NATHAN ROAD

Leave the hotel via the Peninsula Shopping Arcade to exit onto bustling **Nathan Road** ❽, a canyon of neon lined with hotels, restaurants and shops that's dubbed the 'Golden Mile' in tourist brochures, though it stretches away for several miles at least. This whole area of TST fits most people's preconceptions of Hong Kong.

Electronics shops abound on either side of this part of Nathan Road, and off to the west side of the main drag Peking, Hankow and Haiphong roads are also full of small shops and restaurants. Choose shops displaying the Tourist Board's QTS (Quality Tourism Services) scheme sticker.

Kowloon Park

Halfway along Haiphong Road you will find the south entrance of **Kowloon Park** ❾ (daily 6am–midnight). Occupying the site of a former British military barracks, the park is a breath of fresh air for nearby residents and office workers, with lakes, ornamental gardens, aviaries, pools and a sports complex.

The **Hong Kong Heritage Discovery Centre** (Fri–Wed 10am–6pm), which houses a permanent display on Hong Kong culture, occupies two surviving blocks of the old 1910 Whitfield Barracks within the park. Art-lov-

ers will enjoy the open-air **Sculpture Walk**, in the southeast corner. On Sunday afternoons there arc demonstrations of Chinese martial arts here (Sun 2.30–4.30pm).

Leave the park by the entrance beside the imposing **Kowloon Mosque**, the largest one in Hong Kong, recognisable by its magnificent white marble dome and four minarets. Visitors are allowed to enter its gender-segregated prayer halls.

Hollywood East

With the opening of the 'Avenue of the Stars' in 2004, Hong Kong paid tribute to its home-grown film industry. This is the entertainment capital of East Asia, and Hong Kong films and music draw vast audiences from Singapore to Japan. From simple beginnings with crudely shot martial arts pictures in the 1960s, the industry has got ever more ambitious, and its products run from the inimitable acrobatics of Jackie Chan to lavish epics made with mainland China such as *Hero*. A feature of the scene is that its stars – typical of HK – are hyperactive, and work in many fields: Andy Lau, for example, the popular star of gangster dramas such as *Infernal Affairs* – remade by Martin Scorsese as *The Departed* – is just as much a superstar of the Canto-pop music scene. For more on Hong Kong in the movies, see page 137.

Busy Haiphong Road

EAST OF NATHAN ROAD

Continue north along Nathan Road to cross over at the junction of Austin Road, then walk back a little way down the opposite side past the Victorian-Gothic-style building at no. 138, under aged banyan trees – **St Andrew's** ❿ (1904), the oldest Anglican church in Kowloon. Next door, at no. 136, set back from the road, is the former **Kowloon-British School**, dating from 1902. Further up the hill on Observatory Road is the **Hong Kong Observatory** ⓫, another fine colonial building, from 1883. Visits are by appointment only (tel: 2721 2326).

Knutsford Terrace
Carry on down Nathan Road and turn east into Kimberley Road: to your left, opposite the turning into Carnarvon Road, are **Knutsford Terrace** ⓬ and Knutsford Steps, a discreet stretch that is one of the most popular places in Kowloon for alfresco dining and socialising. Good lunch stops here include The Salted Pig, see ❸, and The Yuu, see ❹.

CHATHAM ROAD

After lunch, head east along Knutsford Terrace to join Observatory Road, passing the Stanford Hillview Hotel, and walk down to the junction with **Chatham Road South**. It's difficult to believe, but this junction marked the original waterfront prior to the huge reclamation that

now forms Tsim Sha Tsui East. Turn right and cross over Chatham Road South by the raised pedestrian walkway at Granville Road.

Hong Kong Science Museum
Follow the signs to the **Hong Kong Science Museum** ⓭ (www.lcsd.gov.hk/ce/Museum/Science; Mon–Wed and Fri 1–9pm; Sat–Sun 10am–9pm; charge except Wed), a wonderland of interactive exhibits aimed towards school children.

Hong Kong Museum of History
Next door is the **Hong Kong Museum of History** ⓮ (http://hk.history.museum/; Mon and Wed–Sat 10am–6pm; Sun 10am–7pm; charge except Wed). The collection traces every aspect of the remarkable evolution of Hong Kong, from its days as a peaceful rural backwater to colonial times and the teeming metropolis of today

FACTORY SHOPS AND MEGAMALLS

Head back across Chatham Road and then west along **Granville Road** ⓯, with a few 'factory-outlet' shops selling cheap 'seconds' – overruns of garments manufactured in mainland China for export. There's also a big mix of fashion boutiques and accessory shops here – as well as in the adjacent streets – that makes the area fascinating to explore, especially Cameron Road, Carnarvon Road and Mody Road. These streets on

Nathan Road at night

the east side of Nathan Road are also home to the greatest concentration of Hong Kong's Indian tailors, who produce suits and dresses in record time. Just off Carnavon Road, the second-tallest building in Kowloon, the 64-floor, 261m (856ft) K11 tower (2007), which houses the Hyatt Regency Hong Kong, is also home to trendy K11 Art Mall, on Hanoi Road above an MTR exit.

Back to the harbourside

From Mody Road, cross over Nathan Road once again and head along Peking Road to Canton Road. Immediately on your right is **iSquare** ⑯, a relatively new mall, containing some younger fashion labels, a cinema and restaurants. At the end of Peking Road in front of you will be the gargantuan **Harbour City** ⑰ complex, a maze of hotels and interconnecting malls that stretches almost the whole length of Canton Road.

To end the day, head back to the harbourside and ferry pier to enjoy the nightly fireworks at 8pm, or take the lift up to **Aqua** (see page 112), for some of HK's best bar-stools with a view.

Food and Drink

❶ JADE GARDEN

4/F Star House, 3 Salisbury Road, Tsim Sha Tsui; tel: 2730 6888; $–$$

Right by Star Ferry Pier, with lovely harbour views, this is part of a local chain known for its fine traditional dim sum, served until 5pm. Don't worry if the trolleys look intimidating: there's an easy-to-use English menu.

❷ DECK N BEER

East Promenade, Salisbury Road, Tsim Sha Tsui; tel: 2723 9227; $–$$

A rare laid-back spot, great for people-watching, on Victoria Harbour. It's a simple contemporary (mostly outdoor) bar and snack restaurant, on wooden decking. If coffee's more your thing, it's attached to a Starbucks.

❸ THE SALTED PIG

G/F 1 Knutsford Terrace, Tsim Sha Tsui; tel: 2367 0990; $$-$$$

Traditionally, Chinese cooking uses pork as a base or main ingredient. This, though is a well-conceived and executed European celebration of all things porky – from German pig's knuckle to homemade sausage varieties. Italso offers othermeats and fish for those who are so inclined.

❹ THE YUU

4/F 1 Knutsford Terrace; tel: 2366 2999; $$-$$$

Several buildings along Knutsford Terrace have restaurnts out of sight on upper floors. This Japanese one is easy on the eye in pale wood and has a repertoire of sushi, sashimi, grilled items and hot rice and noodle dishes at fair prices.

Shopping at the Ladies' Market

YAU MA TEI AND MONG KOK

Experience the authentic Chinese flavour of Hong Kong and some of its most fascinating traditions – and pick up some bargains – on this walk through the buzzing markets at the heart of Kowloon.

DISTANCE: 4.5km (2.75 miles)
TIME: Half a day
START: Jordan MTR
END: Prince Edward MTR
POINTS TO NOTE: Potentially a long walk through the streets and markets either side of Nathan Road, but with plenty to distract you along the way, and possible stops. If time starts to run short, you're never far from the MTR.

TEMPLE STREET

Emerge from Exit C2 of Jordan MTR station onto Bowring Street, known for fabric shops and clothes stalls. Pitstops near here include **Light Vegetarian** and **Yagura**, see ❶ and ❷.

Walk down Bowring, turn right up Woosung Street to busy Jordan Road, then head one block west and right up **Temple Street ❶**, famous for its **night market**. By day, the first few blocks are a centre for wholesale jewellery suppliers. If you're thirsty, stop at one of the open-fronted tea shops and try one of the herbal brews. Although stalls open late afternoon, the best time to visit Temple Street Night Market, as the name suggests, is in the evenings (6–10pm), when it fills with after-work crowds looking to bargain for cheap clothes, DVDs and gadgets. You can also catch impromptu performances of Cantonese opera and feast on the little *siu yei* sweet-and-sour snacks from *dai pai dong* food stalls.

Jade Market

Turn left at Saigon Street and continue along past the mix of small shops, *cha chan tengs* (a Hong Kong-style café or diner typically with formica tables and fluorescent lights serving quick cheap food) and roast-meat shops marked by glazed, flattened ducks hanging outside. Turn right up Reclamation Street, with its lively food market (not for the squeamish), to Kansu Street.

Beneath the highway bridge is the **Jade Market ❷** (daily 10am–4pm), packed with stalls hawking everything from top-grade jade to cheap glass trinkets. Be prepared to bargain.

Jade Market goods   *Fresh produce for sale*

If you need a break, head west across Public Square Street to the Broadway Cinémathèque arts cinema (Prosperous Gardens), which is also home to **Kubrik**, a cute café and film bookshop, see ❸.

TEMPLES AND FORTUNE TELLERS

By the small fruit-and-vegetable market on Kansu Street, turn left into

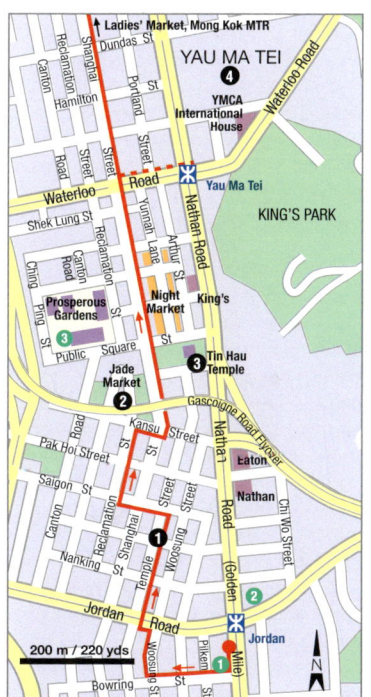

Shanghai Street and walk north to the 120-year-old **Tin Hau Temple** ❸ (daily 7am–5.30pm; free but donations appreciated). The fishermen's goddess Tin Hau is worshipped in the large temple by the main entrance, with spirals of incense falling from the ceiling, an ornate altar with gold effigies and fanciful lanterns. Other temples in the complex are dedicated to Shing Wong, Hong Kong's 'city god', Fook Tak, an earth god, and Guanyin, goddess of mercy. Fortune-tellers, some English-speaking, ply their trade at the south end of the complex, and old men play cards and chess in the park outside.

Fortune-telling

The belief in fortune-telling is as old as China, and fortune-tellers can be found clustered around many of Hong Kong's temples, but above all the Tin Hau in Yau Ma Tei and Wong Tai Sin temple in Kowloon. You can have your destiny read in your palm, your face, or both. All around you, you'll also hear the rattling sound of *chim*. These are sticks of bamboo, each marked with a number and a phrase. You rattle several together in a special canister until one falls out, then hand it to the fortune-teller for interpretation. Other, much more complex, consultations involve drawing up a life-chart for you on the basis of Chinese astrology. You will most likely be asked a whole host of questions for this.

Blooms at the Flower Market

CENTRAL YAU MA TEI

The next stretch of Shanghai Street is lined with shops selling altar shrines, statues of Buddhist and Daoist deities, and feng shui mirrors and compasses. There are also plenty of shops selling traditional kitchen implements, such as bamboo steamers, chopping boards and wooden biscuit-moulds.

Further along Shanghai Street you will find a small park, where elderly men while away the hours by comparing their caged songbirds.

If your feet are tired, turn right at Waterloo Road to Yau Ma Tei MTR station. Stop off for a vegetarian snack, see, or go straight away one stop north to Mong Kok MTR (Nelson Street exit). Otherwise, continue walking north along Shanghai Street as far as Argyle Street. This takes you through the heart of **Yau Ma Tei ❹** ('Place of Sesame Plants'). Although the waterfront has moved about a kilometre to the west, the connection with the sea is still evident in the seafood restaurants, wet-fish trade and traditional artisan workshops.

MONG KOK

Beyond Soy Street, you enter Mong Kok ('Busy Place') – one of the densest urban districts in the world, and once infamous for brothels and triad activity. There's been a concerted effort to 'clean up' the area in recent years, and the 2004 opening of the **Langham Place ❺** complex at the corner of Shanghai and Argyle streets has transformed this part of Mong Kok, with a luxury hotel, office towers, a dazzling mall and a modern range of **restaurants**, including **The Place** (see page 115).

Nevertheless, the old grittiness and street theatre of everyday Kowloon life

At the Goldfish Market   *At Yuen Po Street Bird Garden*

are not too hard to find. New interest in Hong Kong heritage means that efforts are now being made to preserve what's left: just across the Argyle Street junction from Langham Place, a group of pre-World War II colonnaded buildings, or 'shop houses', at 600–626 Shanghai Street are being conserved, while still functioning as ground-floor businesses and upper floor residences. Completion is expected by 2015.

Mong Kok's markets

To reach the **Ladies' Market** ❻ (daily noon–10.30pm), walk two blocks east along Argyle to **Tung Choi Street**, and turn right. Here you'll find hundreds of stalls selling cheap T-shirts, jeans, lingerie, gadgets and gimmicky souvenirs, plus women's accessories, which vaguely justify the market's name. Then retrace your steps to cross Argyle Street and Mong Kok Road to the part of Tung Choi Street known as the **Goldfish Market** ❼ (daily 10am–7pm), where Hong Kong people buy the fish and aquariums considered good for feng shui. The parallel section of **Fa Yuen Street** is lined with factory outlets, and is good for picking up fashion bargains.

At the north end of Fa Yuen Street, cross busy Prince Edward Road West, head one block east, take the first left into Sai Yee Street then right into Flower Market Road, home to Hong Kong's premier **Flower Market** ❽ (daily 10am–7pm).

At the far end you'll find the **Yuen Po Street Bird Garden** ❾ (daily 10am–6pm), where thousands of songbirds are displayed in intricate bamboo or wooden cages, which are also for sale. Return to Prince Edward Road West and head west to reach Prince Edward MTR.

Food and Drink

❶ LIGHT VEGETARIAN RESTAURANT

G/F New Lucky House, 13 Jordan Road, Yau Ma Tei; tel: 2384 2833; $

Lots of dishes based on Cantonese favourites, but in vegetarian form – think noodles, imitation meat dishes – plus enjoyable stir-fries and even vegetarian dim sum. Excellent value for money.

❷ YAGURA

LG/ F Eaton Hong Kong, 380 Nathan Road; tel: 2710 1010; $$

A tasty broad section of Japanese fare in cool, yet unpretentious, surrounds all adds up to a great meal. Add good service, a house label of sake and reasonable prices and it all adds up to a winning experience.

❸ KUBRIK

Broadway Cinémathèque, Prosperous Gardens, 3 Public Square Street, Yau Ma Tei; tel: 2384 8929; $

Packed with books on Western and Chinese film, plus movie-related gifts, Kubrik does cakes and coffees plus a short menu of international dishes for lunch and dinner.

Ascending to Po Lin Monastery

LANTAU

This route visits rugged, mountainous Lantau, Hong Kong's largest island. The Po Lin Monastery and its Big Buddha (Hong Kong's largest Buddhist shrine and the world's largest outdoor bronze Buddha), the fishing village at Tai O and some fine beaches and majestic mountain scenery make it a popular retreat.

DISTANCE: 21km (13 miles)
TIME: A full day
START: Mui Wo
END: Tung Chung MTR
POINTS TO NOTE: Lantau's main sights can be covered in a day, but it's best to start early, and avoid Sundays and holidays. Ferries to the starting point, Mui Wo (Silvermine Bay), go from Central Ferry Pier no. 6.

TOWARDS PO LIN

At **Mui Wo ❶**, take a no. 2 bus to Ngong Ping. The ride (45 mins) takes you past coastal scenery, including **Cheung Sha ❷**, Hong Kong's longest beach, and into the mountains. If in a hurry, take MTR to Tung Chung station, where you can get the Ngong Ping 360 cable car.

From the end of the bus route, walk up to the **Po Lin Monastery ❸**; if arriving by cable car, follow the signs. Founded in 1905, Po Lin's temples and gardens are dominated by the vast, iconic 24m

(79ft) **Big Buddha**. The restaurant here, see ❶, serves vegetarian food.

Ngong Ping Village ❹ (daily 10am–6pm; charges to some attractions) has shops, a tea house and theatres showing Buddhist-themed tales. It is also the terminus for the **Ngong Ping 360 Skyrail cable car** (Mon–Fri 10am–6pm, Sat–Sun 9.30am–6.30pm), which runs to Tung Chung.

If you prefer to keep your feet on the ground, follow the steep trail from here

Tai O village

to **Lantau Peak** ❺, at 934m/3,064ft, Hong Kong's second-highest mountain.

TAI O

Now take bus no. 21 to Tai O. The 20-minute journey passes splendid monasteries, high on wooded hillsides, before reaching the fishing village of **Tai O** ❻, cut off from most of Hong Kong by mountains. Overfishing has led to a decline in the local industry, and most of the dried fish sold here is from the Philippines.

Attractions in the village include the **Hau Wong Temple** (1699), the oldest of four temples in the Territory dedicated to the guardian of the Song Dynasty boy emperors during their time in exile in Hong Kong.

For refreshments in the village, there are plenty of no-frills restaurants, including **Tai O Lookout**, see ❷.

TUNG CHUNG

From Tai O the no. 11 bus will take you to **Tung Chung** ❼, end of the MTR line from the city. If time allows, take a look at **Tung Chung Fort**, built for the Qing emperors in pre-British days.

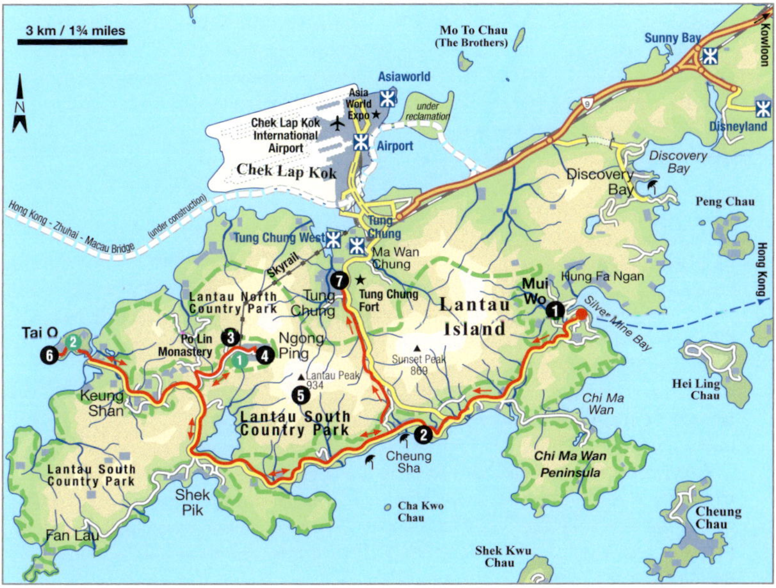

Welcome to the 'Magic Kingdom'

HONG KONG DISNEYLAND

Opened in 2005, the world's fifth 'Magic Kingdom' is smaller than its older cousins in Tokyo, Paris and the US, but for families trying to take in all the rides and shows in Hong Kong's summer heat and humidity, its manageable size might be just about right.

DISTANCE: N/A
TIME: A full day
START/END: Disneyland
POINTS TO NOTE: The resort is a 25-minute ride from Central on the MTR Tung Chung line. Change at Sunny Bay onto the special train to Disneyland Resort Station. For full details and admission prices, see www.hongkongdisneyland.com or call tel: 1830 830. Queues can be long – up to 40 mins – and the best way to avoid them is with the Fastpass system, which enables you to book a ticket for a specific time.

MAIN STREET USA

From the Victorian-style **Disneyland Resort Station** it's a five-minute walk to the entrance. Inside, you'll find yourself in **Main Street USA ❶**, Disney's idealised version of small-town America in the early 1900s. Old-fashioned vehicles and Disney characters populate the streets, and this area has the park's biggest concentration of shops and restaurants. At the **Opera House** you can see the story of Disneyland, and at the **Animation Academy** you can gain an insight into how cartoons are created. Hop aboard the **Disneyland Railroad** to move on to the other themed areas. If you want a bite to eat before you go, food options here include **Plaza Inn**, see ❶.

Food and Drink

❶ PLAZA INN
Main Street USA; $$
Cantonese dishes, including dim sum, are served the old-fashioned way from trolleys.

❷ ROYAL BANQUET HALL
Fantasyland; $$$
The resort's smartest eatery follows an Asian concept of 'four kitchens', serving (separately) curries and stews, dumplings and dim sum, barbecued fish and meats, and tempura and sushi.

A Toy Story Land parade

FANTASYLAND AND TOMORROWLAND

Step through the gates of Sleeping Beauty Castle into **Fantasyland ②**, where characters from *Snow White* or the *Aristocats* wander around rides such as Cinderella's Carousel and Dumbo's Flying Elephants. For respite from the heat, take in the *Golden Mickeys* show, then have a spin on the Mad Hatter's Tea Cups. The plaza in front of the castle is a good spot for watching the nightly **fireworks**. Fantasyland has an international restaurant in the **Royal Banquet Hall**, see **②**.

With the focus on space and exploration, the rides in **Tomorrowland ③** are the biggest hits with older kids: Space Mountain, Orbitron, Buzz Lightyear Astro Blasters, the wild Autopia car ride and more.

ADVENTURELAND AND TOY STORY LAND

Jungle journeys and mysterious creatures are the order of the day in **Adventureland ④**. See the Festival of the Lion King Show, a 30-minute musical that runs several times daily, and take a cruise to Tarzan's Treehouse.

Toy Story Land ⑤ includes rides and meet-and-greets themed around the animation feature's man characters.

GRIZZLY GULCH AND MYSTIC POINT

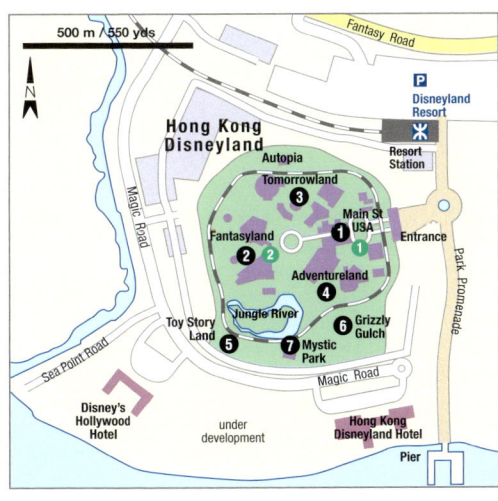

Unique to Hong Kong Disneyland and the biggest draw at **Grizzly Gulch ⑥** is the Big Grizzly Mountain Runaway Mine Cars – a rollercoaster of sorts in which passengers are never sure of its course.

Mystic Park ⑦ is set around the home of fictitious explorer Henry Mystic and his companion monkey, Albert. Dancers from countries he visited perform near the Garden of Wonders, which is full of optical illusions. A ride through his mansion is also full of surprises.

Tin Hau Temple

LAMMA

Leave the metropolis behind and take a leisurely hike across the hills and beaches of car-free, slow-paced Lamma Island, followed by a seafood lunch by the harbour in the little village of Sok Kwu Wan.

DISTANCE: 6km (4 miles)
TIME: A full day
START/END: Outlying Islands Ferry Piers
POINTS TO NOTE: Ferries run from Central Ferry Pier no. 4 to two points on Lamma, Yung Shue Wan (every 30–60 mins), and, less frequently, to Sok Kwu Wan. The journey takes around 30 mins. There is a well-marked, paved path across the island between the two villages. Check the ferry schedule before you start dinner, as ferries back from Sok Kwu Wan can be two hours apart.

Lamma's rolling hills, bays, beaches, easy-going seafood restaurants and tiny villages of low-rise houses (three floors of specific height is the legal limit) are quite a contrast to high-rise Hong Kong. A few Hong Kongers live here: for some, a half-hour commute to Central by ferry is a small price to pay for a car-free environment, where rents are lower.

There's a different pace of life here, and walking or biking are the only way to get about for residents and visitors alike.

You can hire bikes for a very reasonable price at the Hoi Nam Bicycle Shop in Sha Po Village, close to the Main Street.

Watch out on the island's paths for the small motorised trucks used for delivering heavy goods and its toy-town-sized ambulances and fire engines.

YUNG SHUE WAN

From the pier in **Yung Shue Wan ❶**, walk down the bicycle-lined jetty and take a look at the map of the island to get your bearings. Lamma is well signposted, and if you stick to the main pathways it is difficult to get lost. Yung Shue Wan, in the northwest, is the main village. All activity centres around Main Street, which follows the sweep of the bay, where you will find the post office, open-air seafood restaurants, pubs, grocery shops, gift shops and cafés serving Chinese, Western, Japanese and Indian food.

Stop for a dim sum breakfast at the **Sampan Seafood Restaurant**, see ❶, or carry on to the end of Main Street for the bohemian stalwart, the vegetarian **Bookworm Café**, see ❷.

Lamma's seafront restaurants

Tin Hau Temple

Walk for about another minute and you will come across the village's well-tended **Tin Hau Temple**, next to the football pitch. Until the 1970s the fishing communities of Lamma were fairly isolated, and traditions associated with the sea were central parts of local life.

Yung Shue Wan celebrates the birthday of the fishermen's protector Tin Hau (Goddess of the Heavens) in May or June every year, with dragon boat races in the harbour, lion dances and ceremonies at the temple and a week of Cantonese opera in a temporary bamboo opera house.

Retrace your steps back to Main Street, turn right onto Back Street and head south out of the village past shops and Thai, Turkish, Italian and Chinese restaurants, following the signs for Hung Shing Ye beach. Walk through a series of increasingly small villages that give way to greenery, all the while keeping the three chimney stacks of Lamma's landmark power station on your right.

BEACHES

Hung Shing Ye

Hung Shing Ye ② is a sandy, well managed beach manned by lifeguards. As you reach the bay, you'll notice a casual noodle and barbecue restaurant and Concerto Inn, a small hotel with a terrace restaurant. There are various stalls catering to those wanting a few hours on the sand. Pause for a paddle or a cup of herbal tea at **Herboland**, a small organic farm on the far side of the beach. After the farm the path climbs and dips steeply through the grassy hills, above rugged cliffs and small sandy bays. A pagoda and viewing platform mark the halfway point of the walk, and a map lets you see how far you've come.

Lo So Shing

The path descends into a wooded valley at **Lo So Shing**. Bear right through the sleepy hamlet of traditional Chinese houses and right again at the sign to **Lo So Shing Beach** ❸. Fringed by woodland, this pretty beach, with lifeguards and showers, never gets too crowded on hot summer weekends, and is often deserted. It also has picnic tables, making this spot possibly the most relaxed yet well-provided-for on Lamma.

SOK KWU WAN

Rejoin the main path and turn right towards Sok Kwu Wan. Follow the path along the western rim of the bay with its floating fish farms, passing a former quarry that is now partly landscaped. The bay is overlooked to the south by **Mount Stenhouse** (Shan Tei Tong), at 353m (1,160ft) Lamma's highest point. **Sok Kwu Wan** ❹ village is home to only a few hundred people, and is dominated by the many seafood restaurants along the waterfront that are kept busy serving tour groups and junk trips.

All the restaurants are pretty good, and relaxing with a plate of seafood and a cool drink overlooking the harbour is a favourite escape for Hong Kong residents. The **Rainbow**, see ❸, is the largest and best known, and has a website (www.rainbowrest. com.hk) and a free boat shuttle from the Central Ferry Piers (Pier 9) in Hong Kong. More low-key is the **Peach Garden**, see ❹, a five-minute walk along the main strip.

When ordering live seafood from the tanks displayed at restaurant fronts, note that items are weighed and charged at that day's market price, so be sure to confirm the exact price and quantity when you order. Non fish-tank favourites

Lamma Power

One easy way of identifying Lamma from a distance is by the three chimney stacks of Hong Kong Electric's power station, close to the island's most populated northwest tip. This coal- and gas-burning power station provides all the electricity for Hong Kong Island. In a recent nod to environmental concerns, Hong Kong Electric has built one 46m (151ft) wind turbine on the hillside facing Hong Kong Island. The company says it is using the project to gain experience in wind power, and the turbine saves 320 tonnes of coal a year; locals joke that the electricity it generates powers the displays at the exhibition centre at the foot of the windmill. Given its breezy open location, Lamma Winds – as it is officially called – is a pleasant spot to stroll up to and take in the views of huge container ships and tiny sampans on the Lamma Channel, especially if you haven't the time or energy to hike across the island. From the south end of Main Street in Yung Shue Wan, walk for five minutes until you reach a crossing with a wider 'road'. Turn left and follow this uphill for 15 minutes.

Hung Shing Ye beach

include deep-fried squid, broccoli with scallops, minced quail and steamed garlic or piquant peppered prawns.

Mo Tat Wan

If you have the energy and time to walk off a large seafood lunch, consider the undemanding stroll to **Mo Tat Wan** ❻, a 30-minute walk around the flat coastal path. This small village also has a couple of restaurants and shops but is essentially a residential bay with its own little sandy beach and ferry pier with irregular services at both ends of the day. Walk back to Sok Kwu Wan for more frequent connections to Hong Kong Island.

Village fisheries

To learn more about Lamma's people and traditions visit the simple 'floating exhibition' amid the fish farms in the harbour, where fish are reared in underwater cages. The entrance fee includes a short sampan ride out to the **Lamma Fisherfolk's Village** (www.fisherfolks.com.hk).

To return home, catch the Sok Kwu Wan ferry back to Central, or hike back to Yung Shue Wan.

Food and Drink

❶ **SAMPAN SEAFOOD RESTAURANT**
16 Main Street, Yung Shue Wan; tel: 2982 2388; $$
Open from 6am daily, the Sampan serves alfresco dim sum until around 11am – simply go up to the counter, check out the baskets and order what takes your fancy. For lunch and dinner, there's a full Cantonese menu. Enjoy harbour views and taking in village life while feasting. Huge tanks of live fish and crustaceans both entertain and sustain diners.

❷ **BOOKWORM CAFÉ**
79 Main Street, Yung Shue Wan; tel: 2982 4838; $$
Consistently good vegetarian and vegan food close to the Tin Hau Temple. Choose from a long menu of Western vegetarian staples, salads, juices and home-made cakes:

shepherdess pie and veggie burgers are among the more filling choices.

❸ **RAINBOW SEAFOOD RESTAURANT**
16–20 First Street, Sok Kwu Wan; tel: 2982 8100; $$
A local institution, the giant Rainbow is by far the largest of Sok Kwu Wan's restaurants. It's bustling and very enjoyable, with specialities such as garlic prawns and lobster in ten kinds of butter and very reasonable set menus.

❹ **PEACH GARDEN SEAFOOD RESTAURANT**
8 First Street, Sok Kwu Wan; tel: 2982 8581; $
Friendly family-run restaurant five minutes' walk beyond the big First Street venues. It has outdoor tables, tasty Cantonese cuisine and crab, prawns, etc, cooked to order.

Golden Buddhas

WESTERN NEW TERRITORIES

Well removed from the tourist trail, the New Territories stretch from the Kowloon hills to the mainland Chinese border. Within this sizeable area are high-rise new towns, temples and ancient walled villages, a wetland conservation park and Hong Kong's highest mountain.

DISTANCE: Varies depending on route taken
TIME: A full day
START/END: Tsuen Wan MTR
POINTS TO NOTE: The New Territories can be explored easily by train and bus – and inexpensively, with an Octopus card (see page 130). The MTR runs to Tsuen Wan, the KCR West railway line runs from the city to Tuen Mun, and the separate KCR Light Rail system goes around the northwestern towns.

Around 3.5 million people, half of Hong Kong's population, live in the New Territories. Although the 'new towns' spread around the Territories such as Tsuen Wan, Tuen Mun, Yuen Long, Tai Po and Sha Tin are population-heavy, much of the area consists of green hillsides overlooking villages.

HAKKA HERITAGE

The MTR line ends at **Tseun Wan** ❶. Follow the signs from Exit E to the

Sam Tung Uk Museum (www.heritage museum.gov.hk/eng/museums/sam tunguk.aspx; Wed–Mon 9am–6pm) on Kwu Uk Lane. In striking contrast to the modern housing estates that now surround it, this is a Hakka walled village, founded by the Chan clan in 1786. No longer inhabited, it was restored in the 1980s and set up as a museum documenting Hakka culture.

Along the coast road

Now head back to the MTR, and walk through it via Exit A2 to the bus terminus beneath the Nan Fung Centre. Catch a no. 60M or 61M bus to Tuen Mun (30–40 mins). From the front seat on the top deck there are great views of the coast and the Tsing Kau and **Tsing Ma Bridges** as the bus winds along Tuen Mun Road.

In **Tuen Mun** ❷, get off at the Tai Hing Estate terminus, turn right along Tai Fong Street and left onto Tsun Wen Road. You can see the roof of your next destination, the Daoist **Ching Chung Koon Monastery** ❸ ahead, just beyond the highway bridge. The beautifully peaceful temple serves as a home for the

Kam Tin door guardian

elderly with no other means of support. It is also a repository for many Chinese art treasures, including lanterns that are more than 200 years old. The monastery is dedicated to Lui Tung Bun, one of the Eight Immortals, and contains lovely pavilions, lotus ponds and bonsai trees.

MIU FAT MONASTERY

Return to the Tai Hing Estate bus stop, and right in front is the Tai Hing South Light Rail (LRT) station. Take the 610 train for five stops to **Lam Tei**. Cross the tracks, and turn left at the main highway. **Miu Fat Buddhist Monastery** ❹ is on the other side of the road. On the top floor of this imposing three-storey building are three huge Buddhas, and there are plenty more statues all around the complex. It also has a pleasant vegetarian **restaurant**, see ❶.

WETLAND PARK

From Lam Tei LRT station, take a no. 751 train, and change at Tin Tsz onto a 705 train to **Wetland Park** station. The **Hong Kong Wetland Park** ❺ (www.wetlandpark.com; Wed–Mon 10am–5pm; charge) covers 61ha (151 acres) and introduces visitors to the diversity of Hong Kong's marshes. Sandwiched between the high rises of Tin Shui Wai

A crab at the Wetland Park

and the mainland city of Shenzhen, the wetlands can be explored on wooden boardwalks that meander through the park. There are some hides with telescopes for bird-watching, and so far 129 bird species have been recorded, including egrets, herons and the rare black-faced spoonbill. A large visitor centre houses a range of interactive exhibitions on the park and conservation. Should you get hungry, there's **Café de Coral**, see ❷, in the visitor centre.

It's also possible to explore a much more remote area of wetlands at Mai Po, east of the Wetlands Park. The Worldwide Fund for Nature (www.wwf. org.hk) runs regular tours.

HK's highest peak

One of Hong Kong's wildest, most panoramic roads, the British Army's 'Route Twisk' twists and turns in spectacular fashion around its tallest peak, Tai Mo Shan, the 'big misty mountain', which at 957m (3,139ft) dwarfs the 552m (1,811ft) of Victoria Peak (see page 54). To explore it, take the no. 51 bus between Kam Tin and Tsuen Wan, get off at the crossing with Tai Mo Shan Road and walk up to the Tai Mo Shan Country Park Visitor Centre. There are many good, well-indicated walks around the mountain, and in around 30 minutes you should be able to get near to the top, and enjoy superb vistas taking in both the mainland and Hong Kong Island.

WALLED VILLAGES

From Wetland Park station, take the 706 LRT train to **Tin Shui Wai**, and change to the KCR West rail line. Go three stops east to **Kam Sheung Road** station in **Kam Tin.** Leave through Exit B, cross the bridge and follow the footpath to the main road. **Kat Hing Wai** ❻ is on the next, parallel, road, but finding the connecting paths requires a little walking back and forth.

This is the most accessible of a set of walled villages around Kam Tin, which trace their roots back to the 12th century. It was the stronghold of the Tangs, one of the 'Five Great Clans' who dominated the area, a Cantonese clan who moved here from further north around 1150, and built most of Kat Hing Wai in the 1600s. Many of its inhabitants are still called Tang, although several Hakka now live here too. The walled compound has just one entrance, and one narrow main street; inside, many buildings have been modernised, but the way of life is still pretty traditional, and it's worth paying the HK$1 donation to enter. To take a photo of the pipe-smoking Hakka women in their fringed hats, negotiate a small fee beforehand.

Kam Tin's still has a small Indian and Nepalese community from when the British Army's Nepalese Gurkha regiments were based at Shek Kong Airfield. Today the Chinese PLA use the airfield, but unlike the Gurkhas and the British they do not leave the base.

Sunrise at Tai Mo Shan   *Indigenous tree*

MONASTIC GETAWAYS

From Kam Tin, the West Rail line will take you back to Kowloon; to continue the tour, though, head back to **Tsuen Wan** for more monasteries. Once there, walk inland up Tai Ho road to the MTR station. Just south of the station (Exit B) on Shui Wo Street are several bus stops, from where you can get a green minibus no. 85 to **Chuk Lam Sim Monastery** ❼. Tell the driver where you want to go, or just get off when you see the Thai-style shrine at the front of the monastery on the left. It has a lovely hillside location, and the main hall houses three golden Buddhas, around which are hundreds of Bodhisattva statues.

Three temples in one

Alternatively, for a taste of all three major Chinese religions, visit the **Yuen Yuen Institute** ❽ and the adjacent **Western Monastery**, both offering a pleasant escape from the city below. The Yuen Yuen is the only temple in Hong Kong devoted equally to Daoism, Buddhism and Confucianism. The main hall is a scaled-down replica of the Temple of Heaven in Beijing, while the monastery has an eight-storey pagoda. Both are surrounded by halls, pavilions and gardens. To get there, take minibus no. 81 from Shui Wo Street to the last stop.

Eating in Tsuen Wan

If you are hungry in Tsuen Wan, most restaurants are located in or around two big malls just by the MTR station: try **Tai Hing**, see ❸, in the **Nan Fung centre**, or cross the footbridge to Grand City Plaza and **Olive**, see ❹.

Food and Drink

❶ MIU FAT MONASTERY
18 Castle Peak Road, Lam Tei; $
The second floor of the monastery houses a popular big canteen, serving enjoyable all-vegetarian lunches. Noon–5pm only.

❷ CAFÉ DE CORAL
Hong Kong Wetland Park, Tin Shui Wai; no tel.; $
Fast-food Hong Kong-style: this chain has over 100 branches around the SAR. The menu covers Chinese staples, including meat and sticky rice wrapped in banana leaves.

❸ TAI HING
2/F Nan Fung Centre, 264-298 Castle Peak Road, Tsuen Wan; tel: 2498 1608
This branch of the popular Cantonese cuisine chain that is known for its roast goose and roast chicken with rice, sticks to its reliable formula.

❹ OLIVE CAFÉ AND BAR
Shop G4, G/F Grand City Plaza, 1–17 Sai Lau Kok Road, Tsuen Wan; tel: 2412 3836; $
Good-value, tasty European cuisine with a leaning towards Italy. Home-made desserts.

Lo Wu Commercial City

SHENZHEN

Low-price shopping on a giant scale is the big draw of a trip to Hong Kong's gritty young neighbour, but this rapidly emerging city also claims the world's biggest golf club and spa and a cluster of popular theme parks.

DISTANCE: Varies
TIME: A full day
START/END: Any East Rail MTR Station, Kowloon
POINTS TO NOTE: A passport with China visa is required for entry, and it is best to obtain your visa in advance (see page 133). Catch an MTR train to Lo Wu, from Kowloon Tong or any East Rail MTR station. Trains run every three minutes. At Lo Wu, get off and walk across the border into Shenzhen. Taxis are cheap and convenient, but make sure you have destinations written in Chinese and some small RMB notes.

Most visitors head to Shenzhen to shop. Two tips on this: firstly, shops nearly always accept Hong Kong dollars, but you will pay less if you use Chinese renminbi (RMB), and you will need local currency for incidental spending. Secondly, pickpocketing is more common in Shenzhen than Hong Kong, so take care of your valuables and do not wear expensive jewellery.

LO WU COMMERCIAL CITY

Many shoppers get no further than **Lo Wu Commercial City ❶**. It's impossible to miss: cross the border at Lo Wu, and as you leave the immigration building, the Shangri-La Hotel (see page 104) is in front, the railway station and tour-

---

Food and Drink

❶ TASTE

Shop 3008, Lo Wu Commercial City; tel: 0755-8232 1773; $

With picture windows overlooking Shenzhen city, Taste – a meeting point – serves a mix of Western and Chinese food – including dim sum. Does Australian wine by the glass and surprisingly good coffee.

❷ LAUREL

Shop 5010, 5/F Lo Wu Commercial City; tel: 0755-8232 3668; $$

This popular restaurant (expect queues) offers Cantonese food and serves dim sum till 3pm.

Get a made-to-measure suit

ist office are to the left, and on the right is the Lo Wu mall. With around 1,500 shops packed into five floors, it's easy to spend a whole day here. Soft furnishings, handbags, jewellery, electronics, fabrics, tailoring, oil paintings, ready-made 'designer' clothes and a cornucopia of other merchandise are all on sale. Shops selling the same kind of items tend to be clustered together, while restaurants and massage centres (more spartan than spa-style) are grouped around the outside walls.

On the second and third floors you will find both costume jewellery and stallholders selling precious and semi-precious stones, pearls and beads. Many will create new pieces to order.

Scores of tailors are located on the fifth floor. Many speak English or have someone to help with foreign clients; take a garment or just a picture of something you want copied, and then after a brief conversation your tailor will take you over to the fabric market, conveniently on the same floor, to choose your material. Some tailors will make up garments the same day, but if you are having suits or a few items made it's best to factor in a fitting and adjustments and then stay overnight. Simple skirts and shirts can be as little as HK$100; suits and more complicated styles naturally cost more. Custom-made curtains and bed linen are also good value at Lo Wu.

Relaxation and refreshments

After all this hectic buying and haggling, rest and relaxation might be the order of the day, and the Lo Wu can

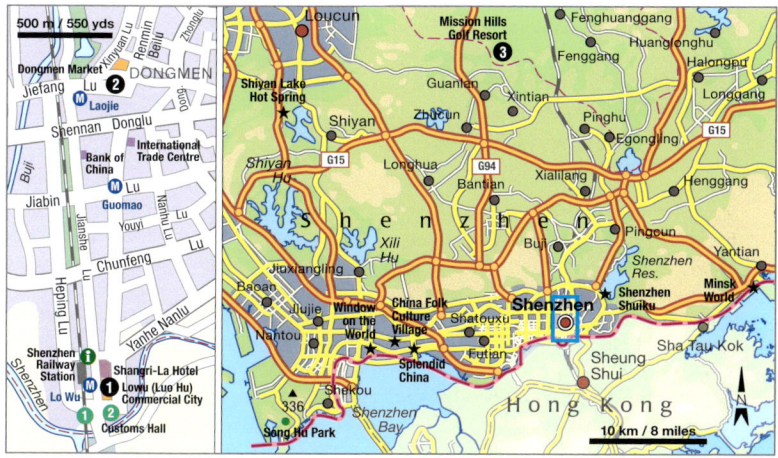

Shenzhen's New Year parade

supply this too, in scores of small massage salons offering no-frills manicures and pedicures for men and women for under HK$50. There are also numerous places offering foot massages or other traditional Chinese treatments.

This huge mall also, of course, has places to eat, such as **Taste** and **Laurel**, see ❶ and ❷.

BEYOND LO WU

Past the border-side shopping zone, the fascination of central Shenzhen is just in the city itself, given that 30 years ago it scarcely existed. A walk of about 1km (0.6 mile) along Jianshe Lu, the main avenue, leads to **Dongmen' ❷**, another shopping area packed with tailors. After dark, Shenzhen is home to a frenetic nightlife scene, spread across town.

There's still plenty more to do around here, but note it's advisable to use taxis to head beyond the centre. What seems like leisure facilities for the whole of southern China are stacked together here, notably several **theme parks** (see box).

Golf

Another thing people come here to do is play **golf**. China's new middle classes have taken to the game, and Hong Kongers play here because it's more affordable than in their territory. There are more than a dozen full-size courses around Shenzhen, plus the world's largest golf resort at **Mission Hills ❸** (www.missionhillsgroup.com), northeast of the city, which has seven star-player courses, a luxury hotel and more. Courses offer packages, and will pick up golfers in Hong Kong.

Theme parks

At times it's easy to see Shenzhen as one great big, peculiar theme park, but there's no shortage of the real thing. There are no fewer than seven fantasy-fun worlds within a 30km (18-mile) radius. Four are clustered together in the oddly named Overseas Chinese Town (OCT), 15km (9 miles) west towards the port of Shekou. Window of the World (daily 9am–10.30pm; charge) showcases facsimiles of everything from the Sphinx to the Eiffel Tower; in a similar vein, Splendid China (daily 9am–9.30pm; charge) packs the whole country into one park; China Folk Culture Village (daily 9am–9.30pm; charge) presents 56 different ethnic perspectives; and Happy Valley (daily 9.30am–9pm; charge) keeps everyone happy with rides and water slides. The Happy Line monorail links all four parks.

Other themed attractions include Minsk World (daily 9am–7.30pm; charge), a 40,000-tonne former Soviet aircraft carrier, located 12km (7 miles) east of Shenzhen. East of the city, near Shenzhen's beach resort of Dameisha, there's also Interlaken Village, a vast park imitating a Swiss mountain resort.

The bright lights of Macau

MACAU: CITY TOUR

An hour from Hong Kong across the Pearl River, this tiny former Portuguese colony is packed with history and culinary traditions – plus gigantic casinos that ensure its role as the gambling capital of Asia.

DISTANCE: 25km (15 miles)
TIME: A full day
START: Largo do Senado
END: Centro Cultural de Macau
POINTS TO NOTE: Fast ferries run pretty much round the clock to Macau, and journey time is about one hour. Turbojet catamarans and hydrofoils (www.turbo jet.com.hk) depart from the Macau Ferry Terminal at the Shun Tak Centre in Sheung Wan. New World First Ferry catamarans (www.nwff.com.hk) depart from China Ferry Terminal in Tsim Sha Tsui. The CoTai Jet (www.cotai jet.com.mo) runs from both Hong Kong terminals to the Taipa ferry terminal, which is closer to the airport and the Cotai Strip. Passports are required, but not a visa. Book ferry tickets in advance at weekends or holidays. Taxis aren't always easy to find in Macau, but the old centre is compact and good for walking. Macau has its own currency, the *pataca* (indicated by MOP$), though in practice Hong Kong dollars are accepted everywhere.

In 1557 Portugal established the first European colony on Chinese soil in Macau, almost 300 years before the British claimed Hong Kong. The next 150 years went by fairly quietly, but things have changed quickly since Lisbon returned Macau to China in December 1999. Then Macau, like Hong Kong, became a Special Administrative Region (SAR) of the People's Republic of China – and its gaming industry was transformed.

Besides the notoriety brought by Macau's reputation as the gambling capital of Asia, the international spotlight falls on the SAR during its annual Grand Prix. The Formula 3 race starts and finishes at the Grand Prix stand opposite the Macau Ferry Terminal, winding its way through 6km (4 miles) of city streets in between. The two-day event takes place on the third weekend in November, so book hotels or restaurants well ahead, if you visit at that time.

Orientation

Macau is divided into the urban area on the peninsula linked to the Chinese mainland, and the former islands of **Taipa** and

In the European-style Largo Do Senado

Coloane. Even the SAR's shape has been transformed by the gaming boom: these islands are now joined together by 620ha (1,500 acres) of reclaimed land, called the **Cotai Strip**, which has a key role in Macau's mission to become Asia's Las Vegas.

Some of 'old Macau' has survived, and has been preserved and restored in recent years. Several buildings grouped as the 'Historic Centre of Macau' were added to Unesco's World Heritage list in 2005, acknowledging the enclave's importance as the first example of European architecture on Chinese soil, and one of the first places where Eastern and Western cultures met.

LARGO DO SENADO

Catch a taxi or bus from the ferry pier – or just walk, for about 1.5km (1 mile) along Avenida da Amizade – to **Largo do Senado ❶**, the old city's main square, paved with Portuguese mosaic cobblestones. The 'Historic Centre' buildings are signposted with green and gold signs, and good maps are also availa-

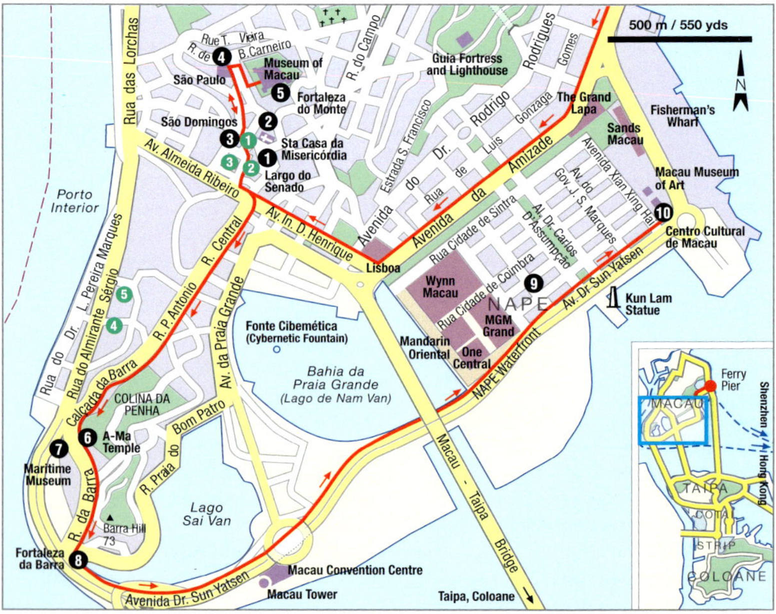

Find your way around   *São Paulo's facade*

ble from the **tourist information centre** on the square (daily 9am–6pm). On the south side of the square is one of the finest creations of Portuguese colonial architecture in Macau, the **Leal Senado**, built in the 1780s and still the seat of Macau's municipal council.

The gracious white building on the east side of the square is the **Santa Casa da Misericórdia** ❷ (Holy House of Mercy; Mon–Sat 10am–1pm, 2.30–5.30pm; charge), established as a charitable mission in 1569, and now a museum. On the north side of the square is the fine church of **São Domingos** ❸. A chapel was begun here in 1597, and the yellow-walled Baroque church was completed early in the next century. At the back of the church is the **Museum of Sacred Art** (daily 10am–6pm), with relics of the centuries of Catholic presence in Macau and South China.

Cafés and restaurants abound around Largo do Senado, so stop off to enjoy a coffee and Italian-style sandwich at **Caffè Toscana**, see ❶, go for noodles at **Wong Chi Kei**, see ❷, or settle down for a French lunch at **La Bonne Heure**, see ❸.

São Paolo and the Fortaleza

From São Domingos walk north uphill to the ramp of steps beneath the **ruins of São Paulo** ❹, Macau's most iconic monument. It was built from 1582 to 1638 as a giant church and Jesuit college, which trained missionaries who were sent all over Asia. Most of São Paulo burnt down in 1835, leaving only the façade, but this by itself is extraordinary, much of it elaborately carved by Japanese Christian exiles.

Overlooking São Paulo is the **Fortaleza do Monte** ❺ (daily 7am–7pm), often called Monte Fort. The structure dates from the early 1600s and still retains its impressive walls and cannons. The **Museum of Macau** (Tue–Sun 10am–6pm; charge, free on 15th of every month), housed within the fortress, has well-captioned exhibits that chart the history of the colony.

BARRA

Retrace your steps back to Largo do Senado, then head southwest, roughly on the well-signposted Historic Centre of Macau Trail. There are a dozen or so churches, buildings and squares from the 17th, 18th and 19th centuries along the way.

Gambling on Macau

Macau has long been the only place in China where casinos are legal. Reclamation around the Macau Peninsula, and most dramatically between the islands of Taipa and Coloane, has provided land for the tiny enclave to expand. In 2006 Macau earned more from gambling than Las Vegas – a pattern that has remained, despite some slowing during the global financial crisis; today there are over 30 casinos.

Macau's architecture is noticeably Portuguese

Located just past the end of the Calcada da Barra is the **A-Ma Temple** (daily 7am–6pm), above the **Porto Interior** (Inner Harbour), which predates the Portuguese arrival. Nearby, the **Maritime Museum** (Wed–Mon 10am–5.30pm; charge, half-price on Sun) traces the history of seafaring on the South China Sea. Some of Macau's best restaurants, especially for traditional Macanese cuisine, face the water along **Rua Almirante Sérgio**; these include as **A Lorcha** and **O Porto Interior**, see and . In this vicinity is 338-m (1,110 ft-) tall **Macau Tower**, with its glass-floored observation deck (daily 10am–9pm; charge).

At the peninsula's tip is **Barra** , a fort that was the site of the first Portuguese settlement on Macau.

NAPE

A hub of hectic socialising on the Macau peninsula is **Nape** , on the east of town near the ferry terminal. As well as several casinos, it contains a number of bars and the **Centro Cultural de Macau** , which has a stylish bar and restaurant. Nape is also home to the **Wynn Macau**, the glistening **MGM Grand, Sands Macau** and the giant luxury mall and residential development **One Central**. Get a taste of Vegas in Asia by visiting one or more of them, or alternatively just catch a taxi back to the ferry pier.

Food and Drink

① CAFFÈ TOSCANA
11 Travessa de São Domingos, Macau; tel: 2837 0354; $$
Likeable little Italian café offering good antipasti, pizza and fresh focaccia.

② WONG CHI KEI CONGEE & NOODLE
17 Largo do Senado, Macau; tel: 2833 1313; $
A traditional-style Chinese restaurant on the main square. It opens late and does delicious bowls of wonton noodles.

③ LA BONNE HEURE
12 Travessa de São Domingos, Macau; tel: 2833 1209; $$
Authentic French cuisine prepared by a chef who trained under the French supremo Joël Robuchon.

④ A LORCHA
289 Rua Almirante Sérgio, Macau; tel: 2831 3193; $$
One of Macau's best for Portuguese-Macanese cuisine: try pork with clams or *feijoada* (pork-and-bean stew).

⑤ O PORTO INTERIOR
259 Rua Almirante Sérgio, Macau; tel: 2896 7770; $$
Delicious Macanese classics in a cosy restaurant.

Fill up at Rua da Cunha

MACAU: TAIPA AND COLOANE

Take time to explore the islands of Taipa and Coloane, south of Macau city. Once sleepy colonial backwaters, they are now linked by bridges to Macau and the Chinese mainland, with the channel between them reclaimed to create the Cotai Strip, southern China's answer to Las Vegas.

DISTANCE: Varies
TIME: A full day
START: Museum of Taipa and Coloane History, Taipa
END: Coloane
POINTS TO NOTE: Minibuses 21A, 25 and 26A run between Macau, Taipa and Coloane. Taipa and Coloane can be explored on foot, but you'll need to take a taxi or bus to get between them.

TAIPA

Minibuses from Macau stop in the middle of Taipa Village. Begin a tour at the **Museum of Taipa and Coloane History** ❶ (Tue–Sun 10am–6pm; charge), near the bus stop on Rua Correia da Silva. The Portuguese only gained control over Taipa and Coloane in the mid-19th century, and even in the early 1900s rugged Coloane was known as a pirates' lair. Exhibits illustrate Taipa's old trades of boat-building, fishing and firework-making, and the islands' mix of Western and Chinese religions and architecture.

When you're ready to see more, step out into old Taipa. Across the road at the junction of Correia da Silva and Rua Governador Tamagnini Barbosa is a small **Tin Hau Temple**, built in 1785. From here head east along Rua Correia da Silva and turn left to reach **Largo dos Bombeiros** ❷, Taipa's cobbled village square. The narrow streets around it are lined with quaint old shops and houses and Buddhist shrines and temples. **Rua da Cunha** is packed with restaurants and Chinese food shops: for enjoyable Portuguese snacks, try **O Santos**.

Carmel and Taipa's old mansions

On a small hill east of the square is **Our Lady of Carmel** ❸, dating from 1885. Walk past the market building, and turn right up the banyan tree-lined steps to get there. From the top of the steps you will have your first clear view of **Cotai**, the reclaimed land that now joins Taipa to Coloane. Over to your left is **Macau International Airport**; behind that is **Taipa Temporary Ferry Terminal**.

From Our Lady of Carmel walk down the hill to **Avenida da Praia**. Before rec-

Eating in Coloane

lamation, ships used to moor along this waterfront, lined with the pretty homes of prosperous Macanese merchants. Five such mansions, built in the 1920s, have been restored as **Taipa Houses Museum** ❹ (Casa-Museu da Taipa; Tue–Sun 9.30am–5pm). Two are used for temporary exhibitions, and three house permanent displays on Macau history and traditions, which charmingly re-create life in Portuguese and Chinese homes in the colony before its boom. The Avenida

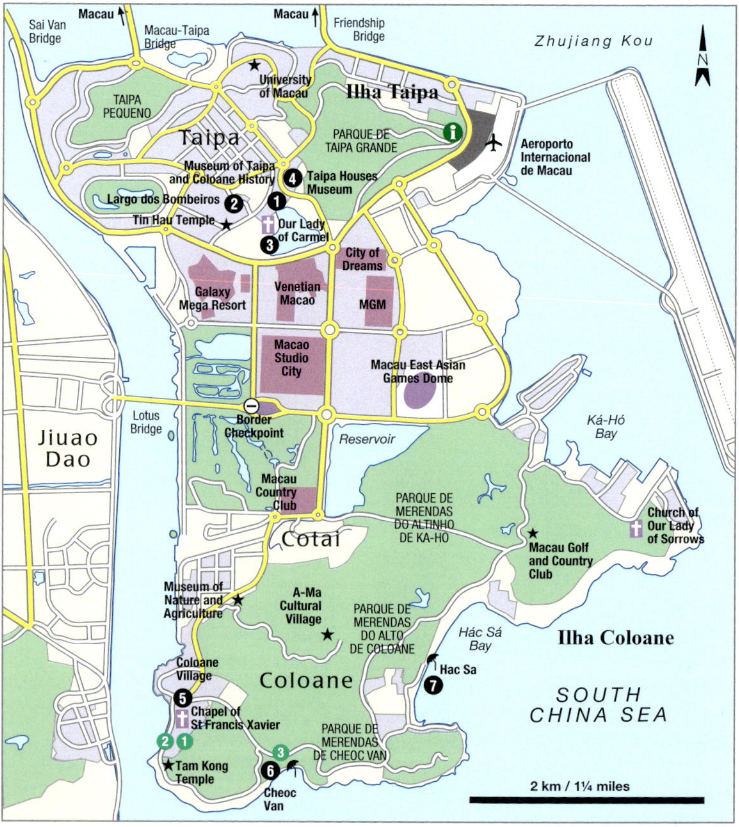

Map labels

Sai Van Bridge

Macau
Macau-Taipa Bridge

Macau
Friendship Bridge

Zhujiang Kou

University of Macau

Ilha Taipa

TAIPA PEQUENO

Taipa

PARQUE DE TAIPA GRANDE

Aeroporto Internacional de Macau

Museum of Taipa and Coloane History

❹ Taipa Houses Museum

Largo dos Bombeiros ❷ ❶

Tin Hau Temple

Our Lady of Carmel ❸

City of Dreams

Galaxy Mega Resort

Venetian Macao

MGM

Macao Studio City

Macau East Asian Games Dome

Jiuao Dao

Lotus Bridge

Border Checkpoint

Reservoir

Ká-Hó Bay

Macau Country Club

Cotai

PARQUE DE MERENDAS DO ALTINHO DE KA-HÓ

Macau Golf and Country Club

Church of Our Lady of Sorrows

Museum of Nature and Agriculture

A-Ma Cultural Village

PARQUE DE MERENDAS DO ALTO DE COLOANE

Hác Sá Bay

Ilha Coloane

Coloane Village

Coloane

❺ Chapel of St Francis Xavier

❷

Tam Kong Temple

Hac Sa ❼

❸ ❻

Cheoc Van

PARQUE DE MERENDAS DE CHEOC VAN

SOUTH CHINA SEA

2 km / 1¼ miles

Lord Stow's Bakery   *Relaxing on Coloane's coast*

is now a peaceful, tree-lined promenade, and the old harbour is a closed-in, lotus-covered pond.

From the Taipa Houses Museum it's only a ten-minute walk to the gargantuan Venetian Macao. Combining a hotel, casino, shopping mall, sports venue and conference centre, all on a vast scale, it's a major attraction all by itself.

COLOANE

Head back to Largo dos Bombeiros to get a taxi or bus on to **Coloane**. What was once the last hiding place for South China Sea pirates is now a green retreat from the SAR's bustle, casinos and construction, with hills, beaches and Macau's only country park. Its resident population still lives in small villages around the former island's shores, and mostly in **Coloane Village** ❺ itself, on the western side.

Around the village
Get off the bus at the roundabout of Largo Presidente Antonio Ramalho. Walk down **Rua Dos Negociantes** to the tiny **Chapel of St Francis Xavier**, built in 1928 to commemorate the recapture by the Portuguese of some children snatched by pirates in 1910 and held for ransom on Coloane.

It looks onto a tiny village square, which comes alive with restaurant tables on weekends and public holidays. The **Nga Tim Café** is also open all week, see ❶. Nearby is **Lord Stow's Bakery**, see ❷.

Coloane's beaches
To see more of Coloane, head back to Largo Ramalho and catch a bus to **Cheoc Van** ❻, where there's an open-air pool next to a white sandy beach. Get off when you see the sign for the **Pousada de Coloane**, and kick back with a long cold drink at **La Gondola** by the pool, see ❸.

Alternatively, go on to **Hac Sa** ❼ (Black Sands), which despite its colour is Coloane's most popular beach, and is home to **Fernando's** (see page 117).

Food and Drink

❶ NGA TIM CAFÉ
8 Rua Caetano, Coloane Village; tel: 2888 2086; $$
Eat alfresco on Coloane's beautiful village square. Delicious Portuguese and Macanese dishes, including grilled chorizo, garlic prawns and African chicken.

❷ LORD STOW'S BAKERY
1 Rua da Tassara, Coloane Village; tel: 2888 2534; $
Well known for its excellent *pasteis da nata* (Portuguese custard tarts) and good for fresh bread, snacks and coffee.

❸ LA GONDOLA
Estrada de Cheoc Van, Coloane; tel: 2888 0156; $$
Spend an afternoon by the beach, then move to La Gondola's terrace for pizzas, seafood or salads with Portuguese wines.

DIRECTORY

Hand-picked hotels and restaurants to suit all budgets and tastes, organised by area, plus select nightlife listings, an alphabetical listing of practical information, a language guide and an overview of the best books and films to give you a flavour of the city.

ACCOMMODATION

Hong Kong has some of the world's best hotels, with suitably high rates. Leading hotel groups including The Peninsula, Mandarin Oriental, Shangri-La and Langham all have their bases in Hong Kong, and international chains such as Hyatt and InterContinental all have flagship properties here. Hong Kong's big hotels are used by locals as much as by visitors – for dining, meeting and socialising.

While scarcity of land means that bedrooms are often somewhat on the small side, the quality of restaurants, spas and other areas, ambience and general opulence of the city's top hotels is hard to beat.

Hong Kong also has a few smaller-scale boutique hotels – with similar prices to the hotel giants – and luxury serviced apartments are another option. There is a good choice of mid-range hotels – some owned by churches and other charitable institutions, such as the Bishop Lei International House, owned by the Catholic Church and vari-ous YMCAs or YWCAs. These places frequently offer comforts – even pools and Wi-Fi. Most upscale hotels now offer free in-room broadband and in-house Wi-Fi connections. More modest hotels in Hong Kong, Macau and China simply offer free Wi-Fi.

Hong Kong's high seasons are in October–November and March–April, when business people from around the world flock to trade shows and exhibitions. Months between these times, including Christmas and Chinese New Year, can also be very busy. At other times, it's easier to find rooms and possibly discounted prices.

Prices in Macau and the mainland are generally less than those for a hotel of the same standard in Hong Kong. However, on weekends huge numbers of Hong Kongers and South China dwellers drop in to Macau for casino visits, so room occupancy is high.

A 10 percent service charge is added on to nearly all hotel bills in Hong Kong; in Macau and China, budget for 15 percent in service and tax charges.

> Price bands based on standard rates for a double room per night, without breakfast.
>
> \$\$\$\$ = over HK\$2,500
> \$\$\$ = HK\$1,400–HK\$2,500
> \$\$ = HK\$750–HK\$1,400
> \$ = under HK\$750

Hong Kong Island

Bishop Lei International House
4 Robinson Road, Mid-Levels; tel: 2868 0828; www.bishopleihtl. com.hk; \$\$
An excellent-value option – owned by the Catholic Diocese of Hong Kong – located 15 minutes' walk from the night-

Great views from a bedroom at the Cosmopolitan

life hub of Lan Kwai Fong, and with SoHo on its doorstep via the Mid-Levels Escalator. There's nothing remarkable about the décor, but it offers many of the facilities of an upper-range hotel – including gym, pool, free in-room broadband, 24-hour room service and babysitter and concierge services – at exceptionally reasonable prices. Some suites have impressive harbour views.

Cosmopolitan Hotel

387–397 Queen's Road East, Wan Chai; tel: 3552 1111; www.cosmopolitan hotel.com.hk; $$

This 20-storey four-star hotel with a contemporary feel is also home to a good Sichuanese restaurant, He Jiang. Guests booking with the hotel are guaranteed a full 24 hours for their money, regardless of check-in time.

East

29 Taikoo Shing Road, Island East; tel: 3968 3968; www.east-hongkong.com

Funky business hotel in Quarry Bay that is a fun place to stay no matter why you are visiting. Tech-savvy rooms have free Wi-Fi. The cool rooftop bar Sugar has a wood-decked terrace with a fine harbour view across to Kowloon.

The Emperor (Happy Valley) Hotel

1 Wang Tak Street, Happy Valley; tel: 2893 3693; www.emperorhotel.com.hk; $$

Tucked away near Happy Valley racecourse, but still only five minutes' walk from Causeway Bay, this relatively small (for Hong Kong) 150-room hotel is nowhere near the height of Hong Kong chic – rooms are old-fashioned plush – but very comfortable, and extremely good value. There's a courtesy shuttle bus to the main business districts.

The Excelsior

281 Gloucester Road, Causeway Bay; tel: 2894 8888; www.mandarinoriental.com/ excelsior; $$$

Around 200 of the Excelsior's 884 rooms have partial or full harbour views across to Kowloon, and overlooking the colourful Causeway Bay typhoon shelter. Part of the Mandarin Oriental Group, this is a huge but friendly upper-mid-range hotel with efficient service and a pleasant environment, close to Causeway Bay's shopping district and the MTR.

The Fleming

41 Fleming Road, Wan Chai; tel: 3607 2288; www.thefleming.com.hk; $$$

When location is everything this 66-room boutique hotel in the middle of the Wan Chai commercial and nightlife district does the trick. Stylish rooms are compact yet cosy and packed with gadgets. Thoughtful touches include a women-only floor and free access to California Fitness next door.

Four Seasons Hotel Hong Kong

8 Finance Street, Central; tel: 3196 8888; www.fourseasons.com; $$$$

Glamorous hotel using light and harbour views to maximum effect, being very

The glamorous Island Shangri-La

close to the ferry piers in Central. French and Cantonese restaurants have won international acclaim. Its spa and outdoor pool are other highlights.

Grand Hyatt Hong Kong
1 Harbour Road, Wan Chai; tel: 2588 1234; www.hongkong.grand.hyatt.com; $$$$
Often the high-rollers' hotel of choice on Hong Kong Island, this glitzy five-star is adjacent to the convention centre and popular with businesspeople and visiting delegates. Its 7,000-sq m (80,000-sq ft) Plateau Spa is on a floor that contains Zen-like spa guestrooms. Fabulous harbour views can be had from most of its modern elegant rooms and suites. The outdoor pool's tranquil gardens belie the downtown location.

The Harbourview
4 Harbour Road, Wan Chai; tel: 2802 0111; www.theharbourview.com.hk; $$$
Affiliated to the YMCA, this smart mid-range hotel – one of Hong Kong's surprising bargains – targets business and leisure travellers, with well-equipped, comfortable rooms and an ultra-convenient Wan Chai location very near the Hong Kong Arts Centre. It's worth paying the extra HK$100 for a room with a view of the harbour, but book early, as it's very popular.

Holiday Inn Express
33 Sharp Street East, Causeway Bay; tel: 3558 6688; www.ihg.com/holidayinnexpress; $$

If you are in Hong Kong to shop, then this hotel puts you in the heart of the action. Rooms are large, with big comfortable beds and contemporary décor. There are no restaurants on site, but there are hundreds within five minutes' walk. 282 rooms.

Hotel LKF
33 Wyndham Street, Lan Kwai Fong; tel: 3518 9333; www.hotel-lkf.com.hk; $$$$
One of the city's hippest addresses, on Wyndham Street, right in the middle of Lan Kwai Fong. The sleek, minimalist rooms have espresso machines and DVD players, and guests can avail themselves of a whole range of services. Dining facilities include a very sexy 29th-floor cocktail bar and supper lounge, AZURE, which is where breakfast is served. Great hotel, although note that the streets outside can be noisy into the small hours.

Ibis North Point
138 Java Road, North Point; tel: 2588 1111; www.ibis.com; $
A clean, no-frills modern hotel popular with tourists. There are 275 rooms with city or habour view and it is walking distance to up-and-coming restaurant and bar scenes in both Tin Hau and North Point.

Island Shangri-La Hong Kong
Pacific Place, Supreme Court Road, Central; tel: 2877 3838; www.shangri-la.com; $$$$

A plush room at the Island Shangri-La

A soaring 17-storey atrium is only one of many spectacular features of the Shangri-La group's flagship, 565-room property. Rooms are spacious, with large bathrooms, a big range of electronic gadgets (including broadband and DVDs) and stunning panoramic views of the harbour or the Peak. Restaurants are highly regarded by local gourmets, whether the refined Cantonese cuisine of the Summer Palace or the modern fine French of the elegantly romantic Petrus. Free Wi-Fi.

Jia Plus Boutique Hotel

1–5 Irving Street, Causeway Bay; tel: 3196 9000; www.jiahongkong.com; $$$$
The stylish, urbane Jia was Hong Kong's first boutique hotel, with lots of the hallmarks of designer Philippe Starck. The 54 studio rooms are compact, but stunning to look at – and the electronics and other services are really state of the art. Complimentary breakfast, afternoon cakes, cocktail-hour wines, gym access and excellent service also make Jia surprisingly good value at this price point.

Jockey Club Mount Davis Youth Hostel

Mount Davis Path, Victoria Road, Pok Fu Lam; tel: 2788 1638; www.yha.org.hk; $
Spartan accommodation but superb views are offered at this famous hostel, with its mountain-top location at the westernmost end of Hong Kong Island, above Kennedy Town and Pok Fu Lam. It's ever-popular with backpackers and hard to beat for value, but you will be required to join in chores. A 30-minute shuttle bus takes you to Shun Tak Centre and Macau Ferry Terminal, from where you are just five minutes from Central.

JW Marriott Hong Kong

Pacific Place II, 88 Queensway, Central; tel: 2810 8366; www.marriotthotels.com/hkgdt; $$$$
A smart, quality hotel with six restaurant choices including the fun Fish Bar, next to the Marriott's great city pool with its dramatic views of Hong Kong's skyscrapers. All of the 602 well-sized rooms have some view of the harbour, and there's direct access to Pacific Place mall and Admiralty MTR.

Lan Kwai Fong Hotel

3 Kau U Fong, Sheung Wan; tel: 2311 6280; www.lankwaifonghotel.com.hk; $$$$
A relatively low-key, boutique-style hotel, with a great location – actually west of the real Lan Kwai Fong district, but not far from Hollywood Road, Man Mo temple and SoHo. There's in-house dining and internet access, and five suites have balconies (almost unheard of in Hong Kong) with spectacular views across Central to the harbour. Very good value among Hong Kong's high prices.

Landmark Mandarin Oriental

15 Queen's Road CentralCentral, tel: 2132 0188; www.mandarinoriental.com; $$$$

The Landmark Mandarin Oriental's spa

With just 113 rooms, this hotel has a boutique feel that spills into its cosy spa and fitness area, with its small indoor swimming pool. The largest guest rooms here are oval with bathrooms at their centre. The MO Bar in the lobby is popular with the local glitterati, and the European Amber restaurant here is internationally acclaimed.

Lanson Place Hotel
133 Leighton Road, Causeway Bay; tel: 3477 6888; www.lansonplace.com; $$$
A modern boutique-style hotel of kitchenettes in many of its 204 rooms that are aimed longer-staying guests. There is a small gym, attractive library-style lounge and Wi-Fi throughout.

Le Meridien Cyberport
100 Cyberport Road, Pok Fu Lam, tel: 2980 7788; www.lemeridien.com; $$
Located in the Cyberport development near Aberdeen, with good amenities and attractive use of technology, this hotel has 173 rooms that are compact but well appointed. Its small landscaped pool garden is very pleasant, and the non-CBD location is quiet.

Mandarin Oriental, Hong Kong
5 Connaught Road, Central; tel: 2522 0111; www.mandarinoriental.com; $$$$
A Hong Kong institution, where the local movers and shakers meet and celebrities stay, lured by impeccable service, superb facilities and some of the finest hotel dining in an already well-served town. The Mandarin reopened at the end of 2006 after a major refit, with larger rooms than before and state-of-the-art gadgets; it still retains, though, its traditional charm. Its famed restaurants and bars include the Conran-revamped Mandarin Grill and the legendary Captain's Bar and Chinnery bar.

Novotel Century Hong Kong
238 Jaffe Road, Wan Chai; tel: 2598 8888; www.novotel.com; $$
Extremely convenient branch of the Novotel chain in the heart of Wan Chai, within easy reach of the MTR, the arts venues around the Convention Centre and Wan Chai nightlife. The hotel's ample facilities include a health club and an outdoor pool.

Park Lane
310 Gloucester Road, Causeway Bay; tel: 2293 8888; www.parklane.com.hk; $$$
Understated and relaxing 813-room hotel, where the bustle of Causeway Bay's shopping zones is balanced out by the green expanse of Victoria Park and the quieter streets towards the Peak. The best rooms have fine harbour views.

Ovolo
2 Arbuthnot Road, Central; tel: 2165 1000; www.ovolohotels.com; $$$
The flagship property of one of Hong Kong's premier independent boutique hotel groups, Ovolo offers designer rooms and a fabulous Central location close to

… and Jacuzzi   *Mandarin Oriental chefs at work*

SoHo and Lan Kwai Fong. Prices include breakfast, Wi-Fi and mini-bar use.

Traders Hotel, Hong Kong

508 Queen's Road West, Western District, tel: 2974 1234; www.shangri-la.com/hongkong/traders; $$

The Shangri-La's mid-market brand has pleasant rooms at affordable prices, to the west of the downtown action on Hong Kong Island. Its 283 rooms have free internet access. Club floor rooms have dedicated lounge privileges. The in-house Café Melacca is a hotspot for Malay cuisine.

The Wharney Guang Dong Hotel

57–73 Lockhart Road, Wan Chai; tel: 2861 1000; www.gdhhotels.com; $$

This medium-sized hotel in the middle of the Wan Chai commercial and night-life district has extensive facilities that include an outdoor pool. Peculiarly, despite it being part of a hotel group based in mainland China, it has a Scottish theme bar, the Canny Man, promising a choice of over 100 whiskies. Other facilities include as Chinese and Japanese restaurants.

Kowloon

The Anne Black – YWCA

5 Man Fuk Road, Ho Man Tin; tel: 2713 9211; www.ywca.org.hk; $$

The YWCA offers clean, simple and spacious rooms at bargain rates in a fairly quiet part of Kowloon, still only a short walk from the Ladies' Market, Jade Mar-

ket and Mong Kok KCR and MTR stations. Rooms are available to both women and men, but there is a women-only floor.

BP International House

8 Austin Road, Tsim Sha Tsui; tel: 2376 1111; www.bpih.com.hk; $$$

Owned by the Boy Scouts Association, this hotel enjoys a marvellous location, in the heart of Tsim Sha Tsui near Kowloon Park. Standard bedrooms are plain but comfortable, although the BP's speciality is its big choice of room types, from dormitory-style bunk rooms to corporate suites.

Chungking House

4–5/F, Block A, Chungking Mansions, 40 Nathan Road, Tsim Sha Tsui; tel: 2739 1611; www.chungkinghouse.com; $

Chungking Mansions is a labyrinth of a building that's home to some 4,000 people, many in 'guesthouses' that have long been a first port of call for budget travellers. Some find the place exciting, others are overwhelmed. Chungking House is far and away the best of its guesthouses, the only one to win the HKTB's seal of approval. The rooms, which are on the fourth and fifth floors (tiny lift only), are plain and small but clean, and all have bathrooms; they're still ultra-cheap, too.

Eaton Hotel, Hong Kong

380 Nathan Road, Yau Ma Tei; tel: 2782 1818; hongkong.eatonhotels.com; $$

Extremely pleasant hotel with facilities and service above the norm for this

The Kowloon Shangri–La's indoor pool

price range – including Wi-Fi and a rooftop swimming pool. The emphasis is on contemporary styling and good value, and prices are very competitive. Well located for Temple Street night market, shops, cinemas and Jordan MTR.

InterContinental, Hong Kong

18 Salisbury Road, Tsim Sha Tsui; tel: 2721 1211; http://hongkong-ic.intercontinental.com; $$$$

One of Hong Kong's most glamorous hotels, with perhaps the best harbour views in town from its grandstand position on the Tsim Sha Tsui waterfront, minutes from the Star Ferry. The Inter-Continental exudes luxury, and its lobby bar and rooftop infinity spa pools are not to be missed. Its superb collection of restaurants is for some the city's finest, with a Nobu outlet, Spoon by French superchef Alain Ducasse and the ever-popular The Steak House.

Kowloon Hotel

19–21 Nathan Road, Tsim Sha Tsui; tel: 2929 2888; www.harbour-plaza.com; $$$

An elegant modern business hotel that soars up behind The Peninsula in the heart of Tsim Sha Tsui's commercial and entertainment district. There's no pool or health club – hence the lower-than-usual prices – but guests can use the sister property Harbour Plaza Metropolis or pay HK$120 to use the upmarket YMCA in the next block. Watch out for its competitive promotional offers.

Kowloon Shangri-La Hotel

64 Mody Road, Tsim Sha Tsui East; tel: 2721 2111; www.shangri-la.com; $$$$

Grand and quietly confident, the Kowloon Shangri-La offers a full range of facilities including a large indoor pool and highly rated restaurants. It's on the east side of Tsim Sha Tsui, and convenient for transport links to the New Territories and the mainland. Free broadband access.

Langham Hotel

8 Peking Road, Tsim Sha Tsui; tel: 2375 1133; www.langham hotels.com; $$$$

Classic styling, sumptuous décor and a choice of seven high-standard restaurants – Cantonese, contemporary Asian-fusion, American and more – are the trademarks of this opulent hotel. It's a snug, restrained haven equidistant from the MTR, the Star Ferry and the China Ferry Terminal.

Langham Place Hotel, Hong Kong

555 Shanghai Street, Mong Kok; tel: 3552 3388; www.hongkong.langhamplacehotels.com; $$$$

Langham Place is part of a multi-purpose office and leisure complex that rises like a shiny new incisor from a once run-down patch of Mong Kok. It prides itself on its use of technology, and the hi-tech rooms have gadgets such as guest phones that can be taken anywhere in the hotel, Wi-Fi, huge plasma screens and DVDs, as well as floor-to-ceiling windows over a fascinatingly

vibrant district of Hong Kong. The softer side of the hotel is seen in its displays of contemporary art, a heated rooftop pool and the Chinese-themed Chuan spa. Its Chinese restaurant is excellent.

Marco Polo Hong Kong Hotel

Harbour City, 3 Canton Road, Tsim Sha Tsui; tel: 2113 0088; www.marcopolohotels.com; $$$$

A deluxe hotel with unrivalled advantages for devoted shoppers, as it's part of the giant Harbour City shopping and leisure complex by Tsim Sha Tsui's Ocean Terminal. Its ample facilities include an outdoor pool and three fine restaurants. It hosts a massively popular Oktoberfest on the TST waterfront each year.

Metropark Hotel Mongkok

22 Lai Chi Kok Road, Mong Kok; tel: 2397 9622; www.metroparkhotels.com; $$

This big hotel offers no special features but good-value comfort and is popular with Asian business travellers and groups. It's in the heart of Mong Kok near Prince Edward MTR, and close to Fa Yuen Street's factory outlets and the flower market.

The Mira

118 Nathan Road, Tsim Sha Tsui; tel: 2368 1111; www.themirahotel.com; $$$

After a US$65-million makeover in 2009, the colourful, youthful and very stylish Mira is one of the many reasons Tsim Sha Tsui's glitz factor is on the

rise. Facilities include the acclaimed restaurants Whisk (European) and Cuisine Cuisine (Cantonese), as well as an indoor infinity pool and spacious soothing spa in the basement.

Nathan Hotel

378 Nathan Road, Yau Ma Tei; tel: 2388 5141; www.nathanhotel.com; $$$

This quiet, pleasant mid-range hotel is located close to the Temple Street Night Market and Jordan MTR, and has 192 spacious and well-decorated no-frills rooms that have recently been renovated. The Penthouse restaurant serves Cantonese and Western food.

The Peninsula

Salisbury Road, Tsim Sha Tsui; tel: 2920 2888; http://hongkong.peninsula.com; $$$$

Hong Kong's most historic and prestigious hotel, 'The Pen' has been a byword for impeccable service and colonial-style grandeur since it opened in 1928. Noël Coward was only one of the globetrotting celebrities who stayed here in its first golden era. Today, one only has to step into the magnificent lobby, where the celebrated afternoon tea is served, to imbibe the ambience of yesteryear. The Peninsula also has its feet firmly in the present: it added a 30-storey tower in the late 1990s, and recently refurbished rooms are the pinnacle of luxury, matching the hotel's helipad and fleet of Rollers. In-house restaurants include Gaddi's, for many

Fantastic views at the Shangri–La Hotel Shenzhen

Hong Kong's best French restaurant, and the Philippe Starck-designed Felix top-floor restaurant and bar, with its men's loo with a view.

Salisbury YMCA
41 Salisbury Road, Tsim Sha Tsui; tel: 2268 7000; www.ymcahk.org.hk; $$
Book well ahead to be sure of a room at this superior YMCA. Rooms, which are divided between singles, family rooms and dormitories, are plain but comfortable and well equipped, and many of them enjoy panoramic views of the harbour and Hong Kong Island's nightly 'Symphony of Lights'. Amenities include a large indoor pool and impressive sports facilities. As conveniently located as 'The Pen' (see page 96), but at a fraction of the cost.

Sheraton Hong Kong Hotel and Towers
20 Nathan Road, Tsim Sha Tsui; tel: 2369 1111; www.sheraton.com/hongkong; $$$$
Busy luxury hotel with a good range of facilities including an outdoor pool with superb views of Hong Kong Island, a Fitness First-managed gym and 'Harbour View' rooms from which you can enjoy fabulous views while lying back in your bath. Restaurants and bars include the top-floor Sky Lounge.

Shenzhen

The Langham Shenzhen,
7888 Shennan Boulevard, Futian District; tel: 86 755-8828 9888; http://shenzhen. langhamhotels.com; $$$$
One of a few top-tier hotel brands to open in the relatively recent Futian CBD, like its international counterparts The Langham is all about contemporary refinement. Restaurant, bar and club lounge all make memorable impressions on the eye and palate. Rooms are gizmo-laden and use luxurious tactile materials. Wi-Fi is provided throughout.

Mission Hills Resort
Guanlan County; tel: 86 755-2802 0888; www.missionhillsgroup.com; $$$$
A very opulent resort that's part of the world's largest golf complex. Its facilities include 12 designer courses, swimming pools and more.

Interlaken OCT Hotel Shenzhen
OCT East Dameisha Yantian District; tel: 86 755-8888 3333; www.oct hotels.com; $$
A few thousand miles and a small leap of the imagination from Switzerland, this ersatz lakeside hotel is 30 minutes east of downtown Shenzhen. There's a huge spa, two golf courses and acres of green hills with a tea plantation to explore. 299 rooms.

Shangri-La Hotel Shenzhen
East Side, Railway Station, Jianshe Lu; tel: 86 755-8233 0888; www.shangri-la.com/shenzhen; $$$$
One of few real landmarks in Shenzhen, the Shangri-La has long held the crown of best hotel in town. The loca-

tion is ultra-convenient, the food is consistently excellent, the gardens offer a pleasant escape, and the 360° Bar, Restaurant and Lounge has great views. Free broadband.

Macau

Altira Macau

Avenida de Kwong Tung, Taipa, Macau; tel: 853-2886 8888; www.altiramacau.com; $$$$

With exquisite bedrooms by award-winning designer Peter Remédios offering great views of Macau plus a fabulous infinity pool in an enormous spa, the Altira is a class apart from the more hectic Macau casino hotels. Appropriately, it's located slightly away from the main clusters. Its restaurants offer contemporary French, Japanese and Chinese cuisine.

Hotel Royal

2–4 Estr. da Vitoria; tel: 853-2855 2222; www.hotelroyal.com.mo; $$$

Conveniently-located upmarket hotel at the foot of the Colina da Guia, in a quiet area close to central Macau. Spacious, comfortable rooms. Facilities include an indoor pool. 380 rooms.

Mandarin Oriental Macau

Avenida Dr Sun Yat Sen; tel: 853-8805 8888; www.mandarinoriental.com/macau; $$$$

The Mandarin Oriental Macau opened in 2010 as part of the huge luxury shopping, residential and commercial complex, One Central. The 213-room property has all the usual Mandarin Oriental comforts, technology and superb service. No casino on site, but MGM Macau, Wynn Macau and the Grand Lisboa are all within walking distance.

Pousada de Coloane

Praia de Cheoc Van, Coloane; tel: 853-2832 8144; www.hotelpcoloane.com. mo; $$

This is a quiet, family-run hotel by the beach. The décor is rustic Portuguese, with blue-and-white wall tiles and terracotta tiles on the floor. It's a lovely place to relax, eat home-style Portuguese food and enjoy the views of Cheoc Van beach.

Pousada de Sao Tiago

Avenida da Republica; tel: 853-2837 8111; www.saotiago.com.mo; $$$$

A great change from Macau's Las Vegas-style projects, this romantic luxury hotel occupies a 17th-century fort, fittingly decorated with dark woods and marble. The garden pool and terrace are lovely, and historic Macau is just outside.

Westin Resort Macau

Estrada de Hac Sa, Coloane; tel: 853-871 111; www.starwoodhotels.com; $$$$

The Westin Resort Macau is definitely the hotel for golfers, with a lift up to the first tee on the hotel's roof. It's handy too for the beach and Fernando's restaurant. A luxurious escape from the downtown crowds.

Traditional dim sum trolley service

RESTAURANTS

Food is an integral part of the Hong Kong experience. *Yum cha* – eating *dim sum* and drinking tea – is a must, as is dining alfresco on one of the outlying islands. *Cha chen tengs* (casual cafés/diners) and *dai pai dongs* (outdoor street-side restaurants) such as those around Temple Street are also unique to the SAR. Dining in shopping malls is also very typical of Hong Kong life; most malls have a mix of both medium- and lower-priced restaurants and food courts, where you order from any of over a dozen outlets, and then eat at a communal table. Some of the best deals to be had at top restaurants are their set menus, especially at lunchtime. The dining areas listed below are packed with places offering great 'lunch sets', which allow you to indulge for a lot less than the à la carte price.

Central, Sheung Wan and the Peak

1968 Indonesian Restaurant
5/F, The L Place, 139 Queen's Road, Central; tel: 2577 9981; daily noon–midnight; $$$

Serving up favourites like *gado gado*, *beef rendang* and *nasi goreng* since 1968, the Indonesian has moved to Central from its historic home in Causeway Bay but remains a destination for lovers of high quality, good value Southeast Asian cooking.

Amber
7/ F, Landmark Mandarin Oriental, 15 Queen's Road, Central; tel: 2132 0188; www.amberhongkong.com; Mon–Sun 7–10am; noon–2.30pm; 6.30–10.30pm; $$$$

A stunning double Michelin-star fine diner with food as creative as the Adam Tihany décor, from the kitchen of award-winning chef Richard Ekkebus. Sample the likes of seared blue fin tuna cubes glazed with soy and maple, and for dessert, caramel, sea salt, and milk fondant with caramelised peanuts. The multi-course Saturday wine lunch here is a treat.

Comfort by Harlan Goldstein
5/F Grand Progress Building; 15–16 Lan Kwai Fong; Central; tel: 2521 8638; daily noon–3pm; 6–11pm; $$$

Chef Harlan Goldstein – holder of a Michelin star for his fine dining restaurant Gold more recently opened this more informal eatery. The menu is international, with highlights including slow-

> Price guide for an average three-course meal for one with a glass of wine:
> $$$$ = over HK$500
> $$$ = HK$300–HK500
> $$ = HK$150–HK300
> $ = below HK$150

Tucking into hawker food

cooked beef cheek on mashed potato, Spanish pork rib with balsamic soy gravy, and southeast Asian beef brisket curry. The pasta and desserts are also great.

Cuisine Cuisine

3101–07, Level 3, IFC Mall, Finance Street; tel: 2393 3933; www.cuisinecuisine.hk; Mon–Fri noon–2.30pm, 6–10.30pm, Sat 11am–3pm, 6–10.30pm; Sun 10.30am–3pm, 6–10.30pm; $$$

Set in a huge, high-ceilinged, highly designed space with indoor and outdoor dining and magnificent views, this Michelin-starred restaurant showcases contemporary Cantonese cuisine with refined modern touches. A second restaurant has opened in The Mira Hotel, Nathan Road (see page 103).

Duddell's

3-4/F, Shanghai Tang Mansion, 1 Duddell Street, Central; tel: 2525 9191; duddells.co; noon–2.30pm; 6–10.30pm; $$$

Unusual for a restaurant in Hong Kong, especially a Chinese one – Duddell's holds arty events, such as screening and talks. But most importantly, it serves top-notch Cantonese fare. Its dim sum and barbecued meats are notably good. Its upper floor lounge is a good spot for a nightcap.

Goccia

G/F 73 Wyndham Street, Central; tel: 2167 8181; $$$

Italian restaurants are popular with Hong Kongers, and this refined one has a superb salad bar and also does beautifully presented authentic Italian dishes. Downstairs is a funky modern bar; upstairs is an equally cool, calm dining room and terrace.

Good Luck Thai Food

G/F 13 Wing Wah Lane; tel: 2877 2971; Mon–Sat 11am–1am; $

Cheap, cheerful dining at plastic tables in a pungent but authentic Hong Kong alleyway just off the bar and nightlife hub of Lan Kwai Fong. Come here to feast on tom yam soup, *phad thai* and other Thai favourites.

Habibi Cafe

112–114 Wellington Street; tel:2544 3886, www.habibi.com.hk; Mon–Sat 11.30am–11.30pm; $$

With Egyptian black-and-white movies playing in the background, and authentic cuisine, this small nook is ideal for an informal meal of tasty Middle Eastern cuisine. For more sumptuous surroundings visit Habibi Restaurant next door.

Jashan

1/F Amber Lodge, 23 Hollywood Road; tel: 3105 5300, www.jashan.com.hk; Sun–Thurs noon–midnight, Fri-Sat noon–2am; $$

Richly decorated, Jashan offers an extensive menu of Indian cuisine, with dishes from north and south. A speciality is the exceptional-value lunch buffet; and there is a Sunday brunch buffet. Fine dining in the evening.

In the elegant Mandarin Grill

Kiku Japanese Restaurant

Shop B 13-16, Basement, The Landmark, Des Voeux Road East; tel: 2521 3344; daily 11.30am–3pm, 6–10.30pm; $$$

A traditional, pine-panelled restaurant serving teppanyaki and sushi delicacies, kaiseki, or sukiyaki or shabu-shabu set-meals. The à la carte menu features Kyoto-style cuisine; great grilled cod and eel.

Life Organic Restaurant & Bar

10 Shelley Street; tel: 2810 9777; www.lifecafe.com.hk; Mon–Sun 7am–4pm; take-away only 4–8.30pm; $$

A popular vegetarian café and restaurant, where health-conscious locals munch on freshly baked flapjacks and alfalfa, in between sips of freshly squeezed passion fruit and carrot juice. Organic beers and wines are also served.

Luk Yu Tea House

24–6 Stanley Street; tel: 2523 1970; daily 7am–10pm; $$

This popular, famous tea house opened in the early 1930s. With its carved wood panelling and doors, ceiling fans, spittoons, marble tabletops, couples booths and stained-glass windows it is fabulously atmospheric. A great place to try the full range of Chinese teas. Also famed for its excellent dim sum (served until 5.30pm). Ask for the English menu.

Mak's Noodles

77 Wellington Street; tel: 2854 3810; daily 11am–9pm; $

If wonton noodle soup is Hong Kong's national dish, this is the place to sample it. Pale-pink, prawn-filled pillows of pastry float on a nest of noodles in a beef tendon broth tinged with fermented shrimp paste. Better by far than its imitative neighbours.

Mandarin Grill

Mandarin Oriental Hotel, 5 Connaught Road, Central; tel: 2825 4004; Mon–Fri 7.30–10am, noon–2.30pm, 6.30–10pm, Sat 6.30–10pm, Sun 6.30–9.30pm; www.mandarinoriental.com; $$$$

One of Hong Kong's best-loved grills, the dining room was brightened by a Terence Conran makeover in 2006. Although the menu is pricey, the Grill is top notch. You may never taste western grill staples this good, such as steak (seafood, pasta and sushi also on the menu), or be treated to such finely tuned service. Book well in advance.

Massala

10 Mercer Street, Sheung Wan; tel: 2581 9777; daily noon–3pm; 6–11pm; $

Friendly family-run Indian restaurant with an extensive choice of favourites. Standouts include bhindi masala, fish madras, tarka dhal and tandoori chicken. The set menus are excellent value.

Nha Trang

88–90 Wellington Street; tel: 2581 9992; www.nhatrang.com.hk; daily noon-4.30pm, 6–11pm; $

Soup at Mak's Noodles

Brasserie dining at the Press Room

Deservedly popular restaurant serving dishes such as bun, beef and chicken pho, grilled prawn rice paper rolls, and beef and watercress salad. Food is always fresh and fast and queues are the norm.

La Pampa

32 Staunton Street, SoHo; tel: 2868 6959; www.lapampa.com.hk/; Mon–Fri noon–2.30pm, 6–11pm; Sat–Sun 6–11pm; $$$

Meat-lovers in the know head to this intimate restaurant for some of the best steaks in town. Aside from tender South American beef, there's an interesting selection of Argentinian dishes and wines, but – as you'd expect – there is little on offer for vegetarians.

Peak Lookout

121 Peak Road, The Peak; tel: 2849 1000; www.peaklookout.com.hk; Mon–Thur 10.30am–11.30pm, Fri–Sat 10.30am–1am, Sat–Sun and public hols breakfast 8.30–11am; $$$$

Located within the developed area of Victoria Peak, this standout building is like an Alpine hunting lodge transported to the tropics. Offers great views over the south side of Hong Kong Island. Vivid, lively and colourful, with a very international menu.

Pearl on the Peak

Level 1, The Peak Tower; tel: 2849 5123; $$$$

Glamorous restaurant with spectacular floor-to-ceiling views. An offshoot of Melbourne's Pearl restaurant, it serves what chef Geoff Lindsay describes as modern Australian cuisine, with creative Asian and Turkish flavours.

The Press Room

108 Hollywood Road, Central; tel: 2525 3444; $$$

High-end casual dining in a stylish, modern European brasserie. Daily specials are marked up on a blackboard, oysters are always available, and great snacks and weekend brunches are specialities. A gourmet deli-café, Classified, is attached.

Ser Wong Fun

30 Cochrane Street; tel: 2543 1032; 11am–10.30pm; $$$

A good example of a traditional family-run restaurant with an emphasis on seasonal Cantonese cuisine. A great place to try claypot rice dishes and snake soup in winter.

Sichuan Da Ping Huo

L/G, 49 Hollywood Road; tel: 2559 1317; daily 12.30–2.30pm, 6.30–11.30pm; $$$

A novelty private dining option, Sichuan Da Ping Huo is run by a married couple specialising in spicy Sichuan cuisine. Set menus consist of up to 14 courses, including Sichuan dumplings in garlic chilli oil, spicy shrimp and melon soup. Alternatively, you can order à la carte for a minimum order of HK$320 per person. The chef may serenade you with a spot of Chinese opera at the end of the meal.

Healthy dining is available at Life

Tim's Kitchen

84-90 Bonham Strand, Sheung Wan; tel: 2543 5919; timskitchen.com.hk; daily 11.30am–3pm, 6–11pm; $$$

Lunch-time offerings ($$) are simple-but-excellent Cantonese dishes designed to satisfy office crowds, while the dinner menu reveals why such a modest restaurant has a Michelin star. Highlights in this clean-lined two-storey restaurant include crab claw with winter melon and pomelo skin with shrimp roe.

Va Bene

17–22 Lan Kwai Fong; tel: 2845 5577; www.vabeneristorante.com; Mon–Sun noon–2.30pm; Mon–Thur 6.30–11.30pm, Fri–Sat 6.30pm–midnight, Sun 6.30–11pm; $$$$

Located in the heart of bustling Lan Kwai Fong, the sleek, fashionable Va Bene is one of the city's most enduringly popular dining spots. It offers elevated trattoria-style cuisine from northern Italy in pleasant surroundings.

Yung Kee

32–40 Wellington Street; tel: 2522 1624; www.yungkee.com.hk; daily 11am–11.30pm; $$$

Visiting the Yung Kee is like taking a 1970s time warp. A true Hong Kong institution, with a rags-to-riches history spanning almost 70 years. Justly famous for its roast goose and the obligatory thousand-year-old eggs. Also great for dim sum.

Wan Chai, Causeway Bay and Happy Valley

An Nam

4/F, Lee Gardens One, 33 Hysan Avenue, Causeway Bay; tel: 2787 3922; daily 11.30am–midnight; $$$

Bringing sophistication and twists to Vietnamese cuisine, the lush styling and well spaced tables here make this an oasis in one of Hong Kong Island's most frenetic neighbourhoods. Regional dishes make up the menu – try the likes of zesty lotus shoot salad, clay-pot clam with young coconut juice, and tamarind mud crab.

Les Artistes Café

1/F Man Hoi Bldg, 98 Electric Road, North Point, Causeway Bay; tel: 3426 8918; $$

Mellow café and art gallery (with a bookshop above), with pan-European food based on fresh ingredients, and exhibits by HK artists on the walls. Homemade cakes are a speciality, and it's a very relaxing spot.

Chikayaki

7/F, Bartlock Centre, 3 Yiu Wa Street, Causeway Bay; tel: 2156 0503; daily noon–2.30pm, 5.30pm–1am; $$$

With its calming zen interiors and plethora of sushi, sashimi and tempura choices, all beautifully presented, this bite-sized Japanese joint feels straight out of Tokyo. Menu highlights are the charcoal-grilled mackerel in hoba leaf and the chicken wings.

Bilingual menus are helpful   *Chef hard at work*

Congress Restaurant

6/F Convention Plaza, 1 Harbour Road,
Wan Chai; tel: 2582 7250; $$$

An extensive international buffet makes
Congress popular with locals and trade-
fair visitors. Choose from Asian and
European favourites and mountains of
seafood. At lunchtime, choose noodles
and salads, to be made to your direc-
tions at open stations.

Himalaya Restaurant

1/F, 20–30 Tai Wong Street, Wan Chai;
tel: 2527 5899; www.himalayarestaurant.
com.hk; daily 11.30am–3pm, 5.30–11pm;
$

Classic Indian and Nepalese dishes
in a cosy venue, accessible up a nar-
row flight of stairs. Food is excellent
value with the lunch buffet costing just
HK$88, including a drink.

Hooray

5/F World Trade Centre, 280 Gloucester
Road, Causeway Bay; tel: 2895 0885; Sun–
Thurs noon–2.30pm, 6–10.30pm, Fri–Sat
noon–2.30pm, 6–11pm; $$$

The sprawling outside patio, with both
dining tables and chill-out lounge at the
edge of the harbour has a great view,
and there are also seats in a conserv-
atory. From the European menu, try sizzling platters of either mixed seafood or
meat – signature mains in winter. Pas-
tas or grilled meat with side sauces are
excellently executed. For dessert, allow
20 minutes for the delicious house
soufflés. Cocktails are inventive here

and change seasonally, but hot ones
are always listed, with extra spice in the
cooler months.

Moon Koon

2/F Happy Valley Stand, Wong Nai Chung
Road, Happy Valley; tel: 2966 7111; $$$

Dine out on classic Cantonese dishes at
the racetrack. Barbecue buffets and a
special set menu are available on race
nights.

The Pawn

2/F and 3/F 62 Johnston Road, Wan Chai;
tel: 2866 3444; www.thepawn.com.hk;
Living Room Mon–Sat 11am–2am, Sun
11am–midnight; Dining Room noon–3pm,
6pm–midnight, Sun brunch 11am–3pm;
$–$$$

Four traditional shop houses were saved
from the wrecker's ball and converted
into this beautiful venue with original
features from local pawn shops. Food
in the second-floor Dining Room is modern British. Those in the know, though,
order bar snacks such as a ploughman's
lunch and park themselves in huge
wicker chairs on the balcony of the first-
floor Living Room and watch the Wan
Chai world go by.

Red Pepper

G/F 7 Lan Fong Road, Causeway Bay;
tel: 2577 3811; 11.30am–3pm, 5.30pm–
midnight; $$$

This long-established Sichuan restau-
rant serves up authentic fiery dishes in
icy air conditioning. For the cautious,

the menu has helpful chilli symbols to indicate how hot the dishes are. For fans of spicy food, Red Pepper's sizzling prawns are a must. No faux retro here: the décor is much as it was in the 1970s.

Slim's
1 Wing Fung Street, Wan Chai; tel: 2528 1661; daily Sun–Thur noon–1am Fri–Sat noon–2am; $$
One of Star Street's great little secrets, Slim's serves up great burgers and much more in a smart, but very narrow, space. It also has a decent range of tasty micro-brews and ales – as well as cocktails – to choose from.

Tamarind
2/F Sun Hung Kai Centre, 30 Harbour Road, Wan Chai; tel: 2827 7777; $$$
A popular upmarket Thai and Vietnamese restaurant. The terrace, which has panoramic views, is great for happy-hour drinks. Punchline Comedy Club (in English), with international comedians, is held here once a month.

Kowloon

Add@Prince
3/F Marco Polo Prince Hotel, Harbour City, 23 Canton Road, Tsim Sha Tsui; tel: 2113 6046; www.marcopolohotels.com; daily 6am–10.30pm; $$$
Do not be put off by the hotel location: this is a pleasant, relaxed restaurant presents a wide variety of food options. You can order from it's a la carte menu

or go for its buffet, served from lively stations that include Cantonese, Japanese and pan-Asian specialities. Hotpots, satay dishes and sushi regularly appear. It is also accessible from the Gateway mall.

Aqua
29–30/F One Peking, 1 Peking Road; Tsim Sha Tsui; tel: 3427 2288; $$$$
A fine demonstration of Hong Kong style, this glamorous bar and restaurant has three separate areas on the top floors of One Peking, all with fabulous floor-to-ceiling views of Hong Kong Island and Kowloon. Aqua Roma and Aqua Tokyo offer a choice between superb Italian or Japanese food, while Aqua Spirit has to be one of the world's most stunning places to linger over a cocktail. Note that they have a minimum charge, however – HK$420 per person for dinner and HK$165 (the rough price of a cocktail) at Aqua Spirit, the restaurant's bar.

Branto
1/F, 9 Lock Road, Tsim Sha Tsui; tel: 2366 8171; www.brantoindianvegetarian.com.hk; daily 11am–3pm, 6–11pm; $
A lively Indian vegetarian retreat with *thalis, idlis* and *dosas* offering great value for money.

Delhi Club Mess
Block C, 3/F, Chungking Mansions, 36–44 Nathan Road; tel: 2368 1682; daily; $

The dazzling views from Felix

A longstanding favourite for inexpensive Indian cuisine, Delhi Club is an easy introduction to Chungking mansions and serves a good choice of dishes. It's always a no-frills but comfortable and satisfying meal.

Din Tai Fung

Shop 130, 3/F, Silvercord Centre, 30 Canton Road, Tsim Sha Tsui; tel: 2730 6928; daily 11.30am–10.30pm; $$

Ever-popular Taiwanese chain with the best *xiao long bao* in town. Shanghai's nationally adored dumpling snack is complemented by staples such as won-ton soup and braised bamboo shoots. There's a casual food court feel to the place, but the quality is superb.

Fat Angelo's

Shop B, Basement, The Pinnacle, 8 Minden Avenue, Tsim Sha Tsui; tel: 2730 4788; www.fatangelos.com; daily noon–midnight; $$

A friendly, uncomplicated, American–Italian-style restaurant dishing up huge portions of pasta that can feed up to eight people. Children get an activity menu, but later on it can also be a romantic setting, with its checked tablecloths and wine served in tumblers. There are five more branches around Hong Kong and the New Territories.

Felix

28/F Peninsula Hotel, Salisbury Road, Tsim Sha Tsui; tel: 2315 3188; $$$$

A top-floor restaurant-bar that's not to be missed, with dazzling views, chic Philippe Starck décor and modern European cuisine. Drop by just for a cocktail if nothing else, but dress smart, and feel like the proverbial million dollars.

FINDS

1/F, The Luxe Manor, 39 Kimberley Road, Tsim Sha Tsui; tel: 2763 8805; www.finds. com.hk; Mon–Sun 6.30–10.30am, noon–2.30pm, 3pm–midnight, Fri–Sat 3pm–1am; $$$$

This restaurant launched in Lan Kwai Fong, but this location is open longer hours, including breakfast. A tasting experience called the Nordic Express Menu plays on a train name, as courses weave between the countries of the establishment's name: Finland, Iceland, Norway, Denmark and Sweden. Not to be confused with fast dining, 2.5 hours is recommended, and it really is an exceptional experience. Whether opting for this or the à la carte listings, top chef Jaako Soursa has pulled out all the stops in bringing the likes of elk pate, a host of seafood and flavoured aquavit shooters to the table. Service is attentive.

Gaddi's

The Peninsula, Salisbury Road, Tsim Sha Tsui; tel: 2696 6763; daily noon–2.30pm, 7–10.30pm; $$$$

The historic Peninsula Hotel's French haute cuisine legend is a high-society magnet, serving flawless food in some

splendid surroundings. Jacket required for dinner. The chandeliered dining room exudes genuine antique opulence. Very fine Continental dishes are expertly prepared and served.

Gaylord

1/F Ashley Centre, 23–5 Ashley Road, Tsim Sha Tsui; tel: 2376 1001; www.chiram.com. hk; daily noon–2.30pm, 6.30–11pm; $$$
This Kowloon institution has been around since 1972 and serves North and South Indian cuisine, with plenty of seafood and vegetarian dishes. The décor is rather on the bland side, but live music is a nightly feature and the lunch and dinner buffet menus offer good value for money.

Good Satay

Shop 148, 1/F, Houston Centre, 63 Mody Road, Tsim Sha Tsui; daily noon–10pm; 2739 9808; $
Tasty Indonesian, Malaysian and Singaporean food including Hainan chicken rice and satay specialities.

Hutong

28/F, 1 Peking Rd, Tsim Sha Tsui; tel: 3428 8342; http://aqua.com.hk; daily noon–3pm, 6pm–late; $$$$
Classic northern Chinese cuisine with a fresh contemporary twist.

Jimmy's Kitchen

1/F Kowloon Centre, 29 Ashley Road, Tsim Sha Tsui; tel: 2376 0327; www.jimmys.com; daily noon–2.30pm, 6–11pm; $$

Wood-panelled Jimmy's is one of Hong Kong's oldest restaurants and has been in business since the 1930s; it now has a street-level restaurant. It specialises in British and European food but also does curries and a variety of other Asian dishes. There is also a branch in the South China Building, 1–3 Wyndham Street in Central, tel: 2526 5293.

M Garden Vegetarian

2/F, Omega Plaza, 32–34 Dundas Street, Mong Kok; tel: 2787 3128; daily 11am–11pm; $$
Popular vegetarian restaurant, offering Chinese-style vegetarian and interesting mock meat dishes. Great value.

The New Sangeet

Shop Nos UG06–08, Toyo Mall, Intercontinental Plaza, 94 Granville Road, TST East www.thenewsangeet.com.hk; tel: 2367 5619; daily noon–3pm, 6–11pm; $$$
'Sangeet' means music in Hindi, and that is exactly what you will find each evening after 8pm, when a Bhangra band plays Indian classics (Indian classics also grace the menu). The décor is modern, however, with moody blues and purples, couches bedecked with cushions, and a certain Bollywood glamour pervading the restaurant.

Nha Trang

Shop OT G51, Ground Floor, Ocean Terminal, Harbour City, Tsim Sha Tsui; tel: 2199 7779; www.nhatrang.com.hk; daily noon–11pm; $

Claypot cooking at Temple Street Night Market

Low prices and dishes bursting with flavour from spices and herbs make this an enjoyable, refreshingly reasonably priced place to feast on Vietnamese cuisine. Recommended dishes include the addictive *pho* noodle soup, fresh rice paper rolls with grilled prawns, crispy skinned suckling pig, and minced pork on lemon grass sticks. Service is patchy, but that doesn't seem to deter the punters. Other branches in Central (see page 108) and Wan Chai are equally good, but this one has the harbour view.

Nobu
Intercontinental Hong Kong, 18 Salisbury Road, Tsim Sha Tsui; tel: 2313 2323; www.hongkong-ic.intercontinental.com; daily noon–2.30pm, 6–11pm; $$$$
Huge views of the harbour and city skyline are on a par with the fine cuts and combinations of sushi at the famed chef's first Asian venture outside Japan. The waiting list is long, but if you fail to bag a table try the small sushi bar with its nine non-bookable stools, or retreat with sake Martinis to the lounge bar, which shares the same vistas.

Oyster and Wine Bar
18/F, Sheraton Hotel, 20 Nathan Road, Tsim Sha Tsui; tel: 2369 1111; Sun–Thur 6.30pm–midnight, Fri–Sat 6pm–midnight, Sun noon–3pm; $$$$
This seafood emporium offers wide-angle views across the harbour and serves a cosmopolitan and ever-changing collection of fresh oysters. The wine list is well chosen, and the staff know their Kuamamotos from their Sydney Rocks. A full Western menu is big on seafood.

Peking Garden
3/F, Star House, 3 Salisbury Road, Tsim Sha Tsui; tel: 2735 8211; Mon–Sat 11.30am–3pm, 5.30–11.30pm, Sun 11am–3pm, 5.30–11.30pm; $$
The house speciality at this famous old northern Chinese restaurant is stir-fried noodles. Chefs demonstrate the art of making handpulled *lai mian* noodles at 8pm every day. The Peking duck is also good.

The Place
Langham Place Hotel, 555 Shanghai Street, Mong Kok; tel: 3552 3388; $$$$
The open kitchen adds excitement to this relaxed yet impressive restaurant in Mong Kok's top hotel. The menu is sophisticated and international – from fresh, light Mediterranean salads to pan-Asian specialities.

Quan Ju De Roast Duck Restaurant
L/G, South Seas Centre, 75 Mody Road, Tsim Sha Tsui; tel: 2316 7218; daily 11.30am–11pm; $$$
A Hong Kong branch of the legendary Peking Duck restaurant in Beijing. Pancakes, shredded scallions and dabs of hoi sin sauce are all added to taste. Staff are highly organised and efficient.

Roast meats to tempt carnivores

Ruth's Chris Steakhouse

108–110, 1/F, Tsim Sha Tsui Centre, 66 Mody Road, Tsim Sha Tsui East; tel: 2366 6000; www.ruthschris.com; daily noon–3pm, 5.30–11pm; $$$$

If you are a carnivore craving a juicy steak, this American chain, serving cuts of fillet, strip, rib-eye, porterhouse and T-bone, should hit the spot. Other mains include tuna, chicken, lamb chops and lobster, and salads and sandwiches are also available. Another branch is in the Lippo Centre, 89 Queensway, Central, tel: 2522 9090.

Sorabol Korean Restaurant

4/F Miramar Shopping Centre, 1 Kimberley Road; Tsim Sha Tsui; tel: 2375 2882; www.sorabol.com.hk; 11am–midnight; $$

One of Hong Kong's best Korean restaurants, serving authentic dishes that draw in the local Korean community. Barbecue at your table or order à la carte. If there's a queue – and there often is – make a booking, then head to Knutsford Terrace for a drink while you wait.

Spoon by Alain Ducasse

InterContinental Hotel, 18 Salisbury Road, Tsim Sha Tsui. Tel: 2313 2256; daily Tue–Sun 6–11pm, Sun lunch noon–2.30pm; $$$$

Spoon is smack on the waterfront in the upmarket InterContinental hotel. A fine French a contemporary menu brings an occasional twist. An excellent wine list is also offered.

Spring Deer

42 Mody Road, Tsim Sha Tsui East; tel: 2366 4012; daily noon–3pm, 6–11pm; $$

There is nothing fancy about Spring Deer, but this Beijing-style restaurant is a local institution for Peking duck, lamb and other northern specialities, and a favourite among in-the-know Westerners and visitors as well as locals. It is handily located too, around the corner from Nathan Road. You should book ahead because it is always packed.

Super Star Seafood

1/F, TST Mansion, 83–97 Nathan Rd, Tsim Sha Tsui; tel: 2628 0339; daily 10.30am–midnight; $$$

An authentic Cantonese experience that is loud and lavish. The dish in demand is the steamed grouper picked from the fish tanks, but anything on the menu will be good.

Tutto Bene

7 Knutsford Terrace, Tsim Sha Tsui, tel: 2316 2116; Mon–Thur 4pm–1am, Fri–Sat 4pm–2.30am, Sun 4pm–1am; $$$

Alfresco dining on a small terrace or garden, romantic Tutto Bene is a little piece of Italy in the heart of Kowloon.

Macau

Aurora

10/F, Altira Macau, Taipa; tel: 2886 8868; www.altiramacau.com/dining#/aurora; Mon–Wed and Fri–Sat 11.30am–2.30pm

Communal dining in Coloane. Macau

and 6–10.30pm, Sun 11.30am–3.30pm and
6–10.30pm; $$$$
Stylish Aurora mixes exquisite modern
French cuisine with a relaxed Australian
vibe. Lounge back on the sofas outside
on the spacious terrace post-dinner and
take in the bright lights of the Macau
peninsula.

Cozinha Pinocchio Taipa
195 Rua do Regedor, Taipa; tel: 2882 7128;
daily noon–1am. $$
Established some 25 years ago, Pinoc-
chio recently moved to a vast two-storey
building close to Taipa's main square.
Food is classic Portuguese, with plenty
of grilled meats and fish. Specialities
include curry crabs, codfishcakes and
mussels.

Fernando's
9 Praia Hac Sa, Hac Sa Beach, Coloane;
tel: 2888 2531; www.fernando-restaurant.
com; daily noon–9.30pm; $$$
With a reputation as the best restau-
rant on Macau, Fernando's offers a
mainly Portuguese menu, with lots of
seafood, including excellent prawns in
clam sauce and casseroled crab. They
don't take reservations, and die-hard
fans wait for available tables at the bar
in the garden.

Guincho A Galera
3/F, Hotel Lisboa, 2-4 Avenida de Lisboa;
tel: 8803 7878; www.hotelisboa.com/
dining-guincho_a_galera; daily noon–
2.30pm, 6.30–10.30pm; $$$$

The first overseas outpost of Portugal's
Michelin-starred Fortaleza do Guincho restaurant, Guincho a Galera does
authentic Portuguese fine-dining in stylish surrounds.

Pousada de Coloane
Praia de Cheoc Van, Coloane; tel: 2882
2143; www.hotelpcoloane.com.mo/resto.
html; daily 8am–10pm; $$$
The terrace alone at this family-run
hotel is a reason to stop here. The bou-
gainvillea-clad restaurant rustles up
everything from grilled chorizo and Afri-
can chicken to acorda (mashed bread
with seafood).

Portuguese egg custard tart in Macau

NIGHTLIFE

Eating is the focus of many a night out in Hong Kong, but there's no shortage of other kinds of nightlife in the urban centres. A massive arts complex is planned close to the ICC and Kowloon Station in West Kowloon, but passions about what kind of dedicated venues should and shouldn't be included, and the final design, have led to the project being delayed. For now, many of Hong Kong's entertainment venues – particularly the larger, government-run, ones – are multi-purpose, and offer mixed programmes of dance, classical and contemporary music, theatre and film.

Theatre, classical music and dance

Fringe Club

2 Lower Albert Road, Central; tel: 2521 7251; www.hkfringeclub.com

Housed in a 19th-century ice house and dairy depot, the Fringe is Hong Kong's foremost centre for alternative arts, with a small theatre and studio, galleries and a rooftop garden and restaurant. The programme includes jazz, avant-garde music and rock, and early each year the City Arts Festival. See page 29 and 31.

Hong Kong Academy for Performing Arts

1 Gloucester Road, Wan Chai; tel: 2584 8500; www.hkapa.edu

The APA, as it is known, puts on courses in every field from television to Chinese opera. It also contains the Lyric Theatre – used by the Hong Kong repertory and visiting companies – and presents fine concerts by its own students and international musicians. It is often used as a venue during the Hong Kong Arts Festival. See page 47 and page 50.

Hong Kong Arts Centre

2 Harbour Road, Wan Chai; tel: 2582 0200; www.hkac.org.hk

As well as containing art galleries and the Agnès b cinema, this venue hosts theatre groups (some in English). See page 47 and page 47.

Hong Kong City Hall

5 Edinburgh Place, Central; tel: 2921 2840; www.cityhall.gov.hk

City Hall contains a 1,424-seat concert hall and a theatre that hosts Chinese opera and Western music, as well as festival events.

Hong Kong Cultural Centre

10 Salisbury Road, Tsim Sha Tsui, Kowloon; tel: 2734 9011; www.hkculturalcentre. gov.hk

Located on the Kowloon waterfront is Hong Kong's premier arts venue, with three fine auditoria and many other facilities. It hosts most performances

On Knutsford Terrace, a strip of more than 30 restaurants

put on by the Hong Kong Philharmonic and the Hong Kong Chinese Orchestra and many visiting artists, as well as musicals. There are also frequent free concerts and activities, especially during the daytime. See page 63.

Other music venues

AsiaWorld-Expo Arena
AsiaWorld-Expo, Hong Kong International Airport, Lantau; tel: 3608 8828; www.asiaworld-expo.com
This 13,500-seat hall has opened up Hong Kong to a flow of suitably giant-scale pop acts. Visitors include Green Day, Muse and Gorillaz. It is part of the AsiaWorld-Expo site and has its own MTR station.

Grappa's Cellar
Basement Jardine House, 1 Connaught Place, Central; tel: 2521 2582; www.elgrande.com.hk
Family-style Italian restaurant hosts a decent range of live music gigs and stand-up comedy. Tickets usually packaged with drinks or food.

Hong Kong Coliseum
9 Cheong Wan Road, Hung Hom, Kowloon; tel: 2335 7234; www.lcsd.gov.hk/CE/ Entertainment/Stadia/HKC/; MTR: Tsim Sha Tsui
Very occasionally, touring bands give concerts at this venue, but this is really the auditorium of choice for local pop divas and some from mainland China to perform.

Hong Kong Convention and Exhibition Centre
1 Expo Road, Wan Chai; tel: 2582 8888; www.hkcec.com
Once the trade fairs are packed up, HKCEC also hosts many visiting live acts: Oasis, Tom Jones and Roger Waters have all played here. See page 48 and page 51.

Kowloon Bay International Trade & Exhibition Centre
1 Trademart Drive, Kowloon Bay; tel: 2620 2222; www.kitec.com.hk
This has seen Manic Street Preachers, Brett Anderson, Primal Scream and a host of other pop acts drop in. Its halls also regularly host touring family shows, especially during the school holidays.

Peel Fresco Music Lounge
49 Peel Street, Central; tel: 2540 2046; www.peelfresco.com
Tucked away in a SoHo nook, this bohemian-style lounge bar puts on live jazz most nights. A mix of free and paid events.

Rockschool
2/F, 21–25 Luard Road, Wan Chai; tel: 2510 7339
By music-lovers, for music-lovers. This roomy venue provides a stage for local bands and aspiring artists. Opens as a pub during the day, so drop in for lunch or a drink and find out what's happening that evening.

Heading to SoHo's nightlife

XXX Gallery

B/F, 353-363 Des Voeux Road West, Western District

XXX, (pronounced 'Triple X') in Western District, is a new location for this underground music venue and club that been driven out of Central by high rent prices. It's the place to head for local and visiting reggae acts and jungle and other sub-genre DJs.

Cinema

Broadway Cinémathèque

3 Public Square Street, Yau Ma Tei; tel: 2388 0002; www.bc.cinema. com.hk

A mix of mainstream movies, foreign and arthouse releases, plus a film library, café (see page 69) and regular events. Hong Kong's first stop for cinephiles.

The Grand Cinema

2/F, Elements, 1 Austin Road West, Kowloon; tel: 3983 0033; www.thegrand cinema.com.hk

This is Hong Kong's largest multiplex, located within the new Union Square development. There are 12 state-of-the-art theatres equipped with 'infrasonic' sound.

iSquare

7/F 63 Nathan Road, Tsim Sha Tsui; tel: 3516 8811; www.uacinemas.com.hk

The new iSquare has two standard theatres, two VIP theatres and a huge IMAX cinema with a 21m by 12m (70 by 40ft) screen.

The Palace IFC

Level 1, IFC Mall, Central; tel: 2388 6268; www.cinema.com.hk

The Palace has five small cosy theatres showing current releases. Smart café, book, DVD and gift shop in the foyer.

Bars

The Backyard

Langham Place Hotel, 555 Shanghai Street, Mong Kok; tel: 3552 3250

Mong Kok's most stylish option for drinks with an urban view. Kick back on the loungers and beanbags and enjoy cocktails by the glass or jug.

Bahama Mama's

4–5 Knutsford Terrace, Tsim Sha Tsui; tel: 2368 2121

Caribbean-inspired bar with a mix of front terrace, dance floor where you can sway to reggae and funk beats, and there is table football for the non-rhythmic.

Delaney's

G–1/F, One Capital Place, 18 Luard Road, Wan Chai; tel: 2804 2880

A popular Irish pub, serving draught Guinness and good pub food. The giant screen upstairs shows rugby and football matches. There's another lively branch at 71–77 Peking Road, Tsim Sha Tsui (tel: 2301 3980).

Dragon-i

UG/F The Centrium, 60 Wyndham Street, Central; tel: 3110 1222;

www.dragon-i.com.hk

By night this restaurant and club is a celebrity hang-out. Book ahead to eat and be ready to win over doormen to party.

The Globe

45–53 Graham Street, Central; tel: 2543 1941; www.theglobe.com.hk

Windowless but cosy with its wooden furniture and whitewashed brickwork, for Hong Kong this is a taste of unassuming Real ales on tap include a local brew or two, and there are bottles too, which widens the choice. Quality homemade pies, salads and more are listed on the menu.

Makumba

2/F Ho Lee Commercial Building, 38-44 D'Aguilar Street, Lan Kwai Fong, Central; www.makumba.hk

For a taste of African culture in Hong Kong, look no further. Above the streets of Lan Kwai Fong, the restaurant/ bar has a performance space with rotating live music nights and occasional drum, dance activities.

Pier 7

Viewing Deck, Central Pier 7; tel: 2167 8377; www.igors.com.hk

Located on the top of the Central Star Ferry terminal, Pier 7's outdoor deck faces the major Central skyscrapers and is open to the public, so order from the bar. Lengthy wine list and wallet-friendly happy hour 6–9pm, with free nibbles.

Phoenix

29 Shelley Street, Mid-Levels; tel: 2546 2110

A charming venue that gives gastro pubs a good name. Extensive selection of wine by the glass and daily blackboard menu. Two-for-one happy hour from 4–8pm daily. Keep on the Mid-Levels Escalator until Mosque Street.

Prime Bar & Grill,

47 Yung Shue Wan Main Street, Lamma; tel: 2982 1688

Take your pick from sundowners on wooden decking over North Lamma's tranquil little bay, or get set for a frame of pool inside or take a seat at the bar counter. This newish arrival to the food and drink scener on this small Island has great appeal.

Staunton's

10 Staunton Street, Central; tel: 2973 6611

Top spot for day-time cappuccinos and night-time people-watching, right next to the Mid-Levels Escalator and busy seven nights a week.

The Waterfront

58 Yung Shue Wan Main Street, Lamma; tel: 2982 1168

Five minutes from the ferry pier, just off Lamma's main street, The Waterfront offers substantial global fare, but it's the view and location you come for. One of the best places to take in the sunset.

Taking in the view from the Peak

A–Z

A

Addresses

Hong Kong is a multistorey city. The ground floor is G/F, the one above 1/F (first floor), and so on. However, the address may also be written '205' (for second floor, apartment 5). Many buildings are referred to by their name as well as the street address, as in *1/F Sanlitun Causeway Centre, 28 Harbour Road*.

Many taxi drivers speak English, but ask your hotel to write addresses for you in Chinese, just in case they don't.

C

Children

Most five-star hotels offer a babysitting service. **Rent-a-Mum** (www.rent-a-mum.com) is a well-established agency that can arrange short-term help with babies and children.

Clothing

Layering is key to dressing in Hong Kong, where you may be switching between the heat of the outdoors and the chilly, air-conditioned indoors, and where, from November to April, temperatures can vary sharply from one day to the next. Cool but elegant clothing ('smart casual') should see you through most social occasions, outside of busi-

ness, where suits and dresses are *de rigueur*. For more on the climate, see page 12.

Crime and safety

One of the joys of Hong Kong is the low level of crime. In the main shopping and entertainment areas men and women can walk alone pretty safely at any hour of the day, and night. Tourists may be more obvious targets for pickpockets in busy areas, but normal basic precautions usually suffice.

Macau is also a safe destination, but more caution is advisable in Shenzhen, where muggings and a few other incidents have been reported – but infrequently. Dress down to visit Shenzhen, and leave your jewellery behind. Stick to busy areas, and when shopping, do not let the lure of a bargain make you forget common sense.

Consulates and visa offices

Australia: Consulate-General, 23–24/F Harbour Centre, 25 Harbour Road, Wan Chai; tel: 2827 8881; http://www.hongkong.china.embassy.gov.au.

Canada: 11/F Tower 1, Exchange Square, 8 Connaught Place, Central; tel: 3719 4700; www.hongkong.gc.ca.

Ireland: Honorary Consul, Heidrick & Struggles, Suite 1408, Two Pacific Place 88 Queensway, Admiralty; tel: 2527 4897; www.consulateofireland.hk.

Elaborate malls reflect the local fondness for shopping

New Zealand: GE01 Central Plaza, 18 Harbour Road, Wan Chai; tel: 2511 7218; www.nzembassy.com/hongkong.
UK: British Embassy, 1 Supreme Court Road, Central; tel: 2901 3000; www.british-consulate.org.
USA: Consulate-General, 26 Garden Road, Central; tel: 2523 9011; http://hongkong.usconsulate.gov.

Mainland China
Office of the Commissioner of the Ministry of Foreign Affairs, 5/F Lower Block, China Resources Building, 26 Harbour Road, Wan Chai; tel: 3413 2424 www.fmcoprc.gov.hk/eng/. Visa applications to visit the mainland are made at the **Visa Office** (Seventh Floor). Two photos are required. Single-entry visas cost around HK$200 to HK$400 (depending on your nationality) and are processed in one to three days. China visas can also be obtained through all the Hong Kong Offices of the **China Travel Service** (CTS), 78 Connaught Road, Central; tel: 2853 3888; another is at 1/F, Alpha House, 27 Nathan Road, Tsim Sha Tsui, tel: 2315 7106, 24-hour hotline 3413 2300; www.ctshk.com. Many other Hong Kong travel agents also handle applications.

Customs

Visitors aged 18 and above can import almost anything for their personal use (including an unlimited amount of cash), but 19 cigarettes, a single cigar or 25g tobacco, and one litre of spirits – wine and beer are duty free. For further details, see www.customs.gov.hk.

Hong Kong has stringent restrictions on the import and export of ivory and other items from endangered species protected by the CITES convention. There are also strict controls on meat, firearms and weapons (which must be declared on arrival and handed in for safe-keeping), narcotics and fireworks.

Disabled travellers

With the exception of the airport, big hotels and some newer large buildings, Hong Kong is not easy for travellers with disabilities to navigate. A useful guide to public buildings and attractions, *The Hong Kong Access Guide for Disabled Visitors*, is available at www.hkcss.org.hk or from HKTB (Tourist Board) Information Centres, and a full guide to transport facilities is on the Transport Department website, www.td.gov.hk. Taxis are often the easiest way to get around, but **Easy Access Travel** has a fleet of adapted buses, which can be chartered (tel: 2772 7301; www.rehabsociety.org.hk).

Electricity

The Hong Kong electrical system runs at 200/220 volts and 50 cycles AC.

There are several temples in Hong Kong

Most plug sockets take British-style three-pin plugs. When purchasing electronics of any kind, always check that the system and power requirements are compatible with your systems at home.

Emergency numbers

Hong Kong
General emergencies: 999 (for police, fire service or ambulance). **Police Enquiries:** 2527 7177. **Hospital Authority:** 2300 6555

Macau
Emergencies: 999. Police: 919.

Shenzhen
Police: 110. Fire services: 119. Ambulance: 120

Gay and lesbian travellers

Hong Kong's gay scene may not yet have come of age, but it had its long-overdue coming-out party with its first Pink Parade in October 2004 (there have been subsequent ones), and the city's Gay and Lesbian Film Festival has become part of the alternative arts calendar. For information on events and happenings, see Pink Season (www.pinkseason.hk), look for *HK Magazine* and Saturday night radio programme The Gaybourhood, on RTHK Radio 3 (www.rthk.hk).

One staple of the local scene is Club 97 in Lan Kwai Fong on a Friday night.

Health

No vaccinations are required to enter Hong Kong, but doctors often recommend immunisations against hepatitis A and B, flu, polio and tetanus. Tap water exceeds WHO standards, but bottled water may be more palatable and is widely available. For current information on influenza and other health concerns, see www.who.int/csr/en.

Medical services
All visitors are strongly advised to take out adequate travel health insurance before arriving, to cover emergencies and all other possible medical expenses. Hong Kong does not have a free national health care system, and visitors are required to pay at least HK$990 if they use the Accident & Emergency services at public hospitals. Listed below are some hospitals with 24-hour A&E services. For more information on all medical services, call the Hospital Authority helpline, tel: 2300 6555, or visit www.ha.org.hk.

Hospitals
Caritas Medical Centre: 111 Wing Hong Street, Sham Sui Po, Kowloon; tel: 3408 7911.
Prince of Wales Hospital: 30–32 Ngan Shing Street, Sha Tin, New Territories; tel: 2632 2211.
Queen Elizabeth Hospital: 30 Gascoigne Road, Kowloon; tel: 2958 8888.

Hong Kong is a high-rise city

Queen Mary Hospital: 102 Pok Fu Lam Road, near Aberdeen, Hong Kong Island; tel: 2255 3838.

Macau
Kiang Wu Hospital, Estr. Coelho do Amaral; tel: 2837 1333.
S. Januário Hospital, Estr. do Visconde de S. Januário; tel: 2831 3731.

Shenzhen
Shenzhen People's Hospital, 1017 Dongmen Bei Lu; tel: 2553 3018.

Pharmacies
Conventional pharmacies (identified by a red cross) are abundant in Hong Kong and Macau, as are traditional Chinese herbalists. Pharmacies will only accept prescriptions issued by a doctor in Hong Kong.

Holidays

Hong Kong's public holidays are a mixture of traditional Chinese, Christian and political feast days. Banks, offices, post offices and some shops will all be closed on the following:
1 Jan: New Year's Day
Late Jan/Feb: Chinese (Lunar) New Year, a three-day holiday
Mar/Apr: Good Friday and Easter Monday
Mar/Apr: Ching Ming Festival
Apr/May: Buddha's Birthday
1 May: Labour Day
June: Tuen Ng (Dragon Boat) Festival
1 July: Hong Kong Special Administrative Region Establishment Day
Sept: the day following the Mid-Autumn Festival
1 Oct: China National Day
Oct: Chung Yeung Festival
25 Dec: Christmas Day. The 26th, or the first weekday after Christmas Day, is also a holiday.

Macau
As Hong Kong, but with some additional days:
1–2 Oct: National Day
2 Nov: All Souls' Day
8 Dec: Feast of the Immaculate Conception
22 Dec: Winter Solstice
20 Dec: Macau SAR Establishment Day

China
1 Jan: New Year's Day
Late Jan/Feb: Chinese (Lunar) New Year, nearly all offices, banks and government departments close for a full week.
Mar/Apr: Ching Ming Festival
1 May: Labour Day, plus two following days
June: Tuen Ng (Dragon Boat) Festival
Sept: Mid-Autumn Festival
1 Oct: China National Day; officially three days but nearly all offices, banks and government departments close for a full week.

Hours

Offices generally open Mon to Fri 9am–

5.30pm or 6pm, but some government offices open from 8.30am–4.30pm. Many business offices also work a half-day (9am–1pm) on Sat. Banks are open Mon to Fri 9am–4.30pm, Sat 9am–12.30pm.

Mall shopping tends to go on daily between 10am and 9pm, but the major shopping districts of Causeway Bay and Tsim Sha Tsui stay open later, till 10 or 11pm. Smaller local shops, especially for food, open earlier, at 8–9am daily, and each market is different: some open mainly in the morning, while others, such as Yau Ma Tei's famous Temple Street night market, don't get going until late afternoon.

I

ID

Hong Kong residents are required to carry an identity card. Visitors are advised to carry with them a similar form of photo identification, such as your passport or a photocopy of it.

Internet

All hotels provide internet access, in public areas, though many will charge for in-room service. Free wireless broadband access (Wi-Fi) is becoming more widespread all the time in hotels, and the government is building a free city-wide GovWiFi network – it already exists in public libraries. You can also access the web for free at PCs in many coffee shops.

L

Left luggage

Facilities are available at Hong Kong Airport, and in Kowloon at Hung Hom Station and the Hong Kong China City Building.

Lost property

To report lost or stolen property, contact the Hong Kong Police. Call 2860 2000 to find out the location of the nearest police station. If you are think you left your property in a taxi, it may be worth contacting the taxi lost property line which will – in theory at least, and for a charge – inform all taxi drivers. Tel: 1872 920.

M

Maps

HKTB Information Centres (see page 128) carry an extensive range of maps and give them to visitors on arrival. The General Post Office, 2 Connaught Road, has a good choice of maps and guides in its ground-floor gift shop.

Money

The currency unit is the Hong Kong Dollar, which is pegged to the US dollar at around US$1 = HK$7.80. In early 2014 HK dollar exchange rates were HK$12.60 to £1 sterling or HK$10.50 to E1.

Bank notes are issued by HSBC, Standard Chartered Bank and the Bank

of China in the following denominations: HK$1,000, HK$500, HK$100, HK$50, HK$20 and the plasticised HK$10. Coins include HK$10, HK$5, HK$2, HK$1, 50 cents, 20 cents and 10 cents.

Hong Kong dollars are interchangeable with the Macau currency, the Patacca (MOP).

In Shenzhen, Lo Wu stores will accept Hong Kong dollars and convert to Renminbi (RMB) on the spot, but taxis and other retailers want to be paid in RMP, so it may be worth changing your money before crossing the border In early 2014, HK$1 = RMB 0.80.

Traveller's cheques

Banks, hotels and money changers accept traveller's cheques. Banks generally offer the best rates to change them (also foreign currency), although most charge commission.

Credit cards and ATMs

Visa, MasterCard, American Express and other major cards are accepted at most hotels, restaurants and shops. However, check the cash price in shops; it may be lower than for card purchases. In most street markets, only cash is accepted. When using cards, check that the total is filled in correctly, and keep the customer's copy.

Cash Machines (ATMs) are plentiful. Visa and MasterCard holders can get HK dollars from Hang Seng Bank and HSBC cash machines; American Express cardholders can access Jetco ATMs.

Tipping

Tipping is customary in Hong Kong in bars, restaurants and hotels. A ten percent service charge is added to the bill in many restaurants, but it is still customary to add a further five percent to go direct to the staff. Taxi drivers do not expect to be tipped, but rounding up the fare to the nearest dollar or two is appreciated.

In places frequented by tourists in Macau and Shenzhen tipping is increasingly common practice; follow the same guidelines as in Hong Kong.

P

Post

The Hong Kong mail is fast and efficient. Stamps are normally bought at post offices, most of which open Mon–Fri 9am–5pm, and Sat mornings. Airmail stamps are also available at 7–11 and Circle-K convenience stores. For more information, visit www.hongkongpost.com.

T

Telephones

Public telephone kiosks, although not as common as they once were, can still be found all around Hong Kong – the easiest places to find them are MTR stations, 7–11 stores and hotel and bank lobbies. The standard charge for using a pay phone is HK$1 per five minutes for local calls. However, Hong Kong landline local calls are free, so you can usu-

ally use a phone in a shop or restaurant for no charge. (Note, though, that many hotels charge for local calls from your hotel room.)

You can make international calls direct from pay phones with a credit card or stored-value phone card (available at HKTB Information Centres, 7–11s and some bookshops). To make a call outside Hong Kong, dial the international access code, 001, followed by the country code and number. Within Hong Kong, there are no area codes and all numbers have eight digits, except for toll-free numbers, which begin with 800, and some public information numbers, which begin with 18 or 10.

Mobile (cell) phones

Hong Kongers love their mobile phones. Most providers' phone systems (GSM 900, PCS 1800, CDMA, WCDMA operate in Hong Kong. To avoid roaming charges, it's a good idea to get a pre-paid SIM card with a Hong Kong number and fixed number of minutes. Many phone providers and convenience stores sell SIM cards.

Telephone codes
Hong Kong from abroad **852**
Macau **853**
Mainland China **86**
Shenzhen **86 755**

Useful phone numbers
Hong Kong Directory Enquiries: **1081**
International Directory Enquiries: **10013**
International Operator/Collect calls: **10010**
Hong Kong International Airport Information, in English (24 hours): **2181 0000**
Weather Information: **187 8200**

Time

Hong Kong is eight hours ahead of GMT and 13 hours ahead of US Eastern Time. Unlike in Europe and the US, there is no daylight saving time, so from April to October the difference is reduced to seven hours ahead of London and 12 ahead of New York.

Tourist information

The Hong Kong Tourist Board (HKTB) has booths at the airport, some ferry piers and at land crossings just after you clear customs. They offer free HKTB information packs, which contain a map, a current-events magazine, brochures and details of tourist-board-organised day and half-day tours. They also run an excellent multilingual visitor hotline, tel: 2508 1234 (daily 8am–6pm), and have a great website: www.discoverhong kong.com.
Other useful websites include:
Hong Kong SAR Leisure and Culture Department: www.lcsd.gov.hk.
Macau Tourist Office: www.macau tourism.gov.mo.

HKTB Information Centres
Hong Kong International Airport: Transfer Area E2 and Buffer Halls A and B, Arrivals Level, Terminal 1; daily 8am–9pm.
Hong Kong Island: The Peak Piazza;

In Man Mo Temple

daily 9am–9pm.
Kowloon: Star Ferry Concourse, Tsim Sha Tsui; daily 8am–8pm.

Tours

The HKTB offers a varied mix of tours, bookable from its Information Centres. Other attractive options include: New World First Bus's day's unlimited hop-on hop-off rides (HK$50 per day; HK$25, concessions) on its two open-top Rickshaw Bus routes on Hong Kong Island (www.nwstbus.com.hk). HeliExpress (tel: 2108 9898; www.helihongkong.com) offer day and night sightseeing tours by helicopter. Hong Kong Dolphinwatch (tel: 2984 1414; www.hkdolphinwatch.com) runs regular half-day trips to see the Pearl River's endangered dolphins off Lantau. Saffron Cruises (tel: 2857 1311; www.saffron-cruises.com) has Chinese junks and other boats for hire. Watertours of HK (tel: 2926 3868; www.watertours.com.hk) offer a choice of nine harbour cruises in delightfully gaudy boats, in the morning, afternoon or by night.

Transport

The high-rise jungles of Hong Kong may look daunting, but this is an easy city to get around, thanks to a highly efficient, easy-to-use public transport system. To make the most of it (and save money), use an Octopus travel card or a Transport Pass (see page 130) rather than single tickets. Children aged under 11 travel half-fare on most transport, and under-3s travel free.

Arriving by air

Hong Kong International Airport (HKIA) is at Chek Lap Kok, on the north shore of Lantau Island about 34km (21 miles) from Central, which, as its name suggests, is the urban heart of Hong Kong Island. Immigration queues are dealt with swiftly, and suitcases are often circling the carousel by the time you reach the baggage hall.

Airport Information: tel: 2181 0000; www.hongkongairport.com.

Transport to and from the airport

All transport to the city leaves from the Ground Transportation Centre, well signposted from the Arrivals Hall. The Airport Express rail line, part of the MTR system (see opposite), is the quickest and most convenient, but not the cheapest, way into town. All trains now run to and from the AsiaWorld-Expo exhibition site beside the airport as well as from the Transportation Centre, and reach Central station in just 23 minutes, with stops at Tsing Yi and Kowloon.

Trains run in both directions daily 5.50am–1.15am, every 12 minutes. Tickets to Central cost HK$100 single, HK$180 return, to Kowloon HK$90 single, HK$160 return, but note that you can already use an Octopus card (see page 130) to save money from the airport. Tourists can buy a three-day pass inclusive of either a single or return Airpost Express journey, plus three days of unlimited travel on MTR, Light Railway and bus, for HK$220 and HK$300, respectively.

Airport Express connects with the MTR at Tsing Yi and Central. Free shuttle buses also run between Central and Kowloon Airport Express stations and many hotels, Hung Hom MTR train station and the China Ferry Terminal. Passengers can check in bags at Airport Express stations up to two hours before departure.

Travellers leaving Hong Kong can check in their luggage at the airline counters at the Airport Express stations at Hong Kong Central and Kowloon up to a full day before their flight time with most airlines.

There are also airport buses, which run to every part of Hong Kong and the New Territories. Airbus services, prefixed A, run to various destinations, and there are also slower, still cheaper 'commuter' buses (prefixed E). A11 and A12 run through the busiest parts of Hong Kong Island, A21 through Kowloon. Airbus fares to the city start at HK$40, while E-route fares start at HK$21. Route details are posted at the Transportation Centre.

There are also shuttle buses to Tung Chung station on the main MTR, which is cheaper than Airport Express. Night buses from the airport (prefixed N) mostly run from around 0.20–5am.

Taxis are easy to find, at the rank outside the Ground Transportation Centre. Urban taxis are red; New Territories taxis are green; local Lantau taxis are blue. A taxi to Central on Hong Kong Island will cost around HK$350, to Kowloon slightly less; all fares from the airport include HK$30 toll for the Lantau island road bridge.

Arriving by sea
Macau and a handful of cities in Guangdong, China are connected to Hong Kong by ferry. Hong Kong is also a starting-off or end point to a large number of cruise itineraries. For now, cruise ships dock at the **Ocean Terminal** in Tsim Sha Tsui, right next to the Harbour City mall. A new cruise terminal is opened in 2013 at the site of the former airport at Kai Tak; it is still in its infancy.

Getting around: travel passes
The **Octopus card** is a smart card, valid on all kinds of transport except taxis and some minibuses and ferries. It can be bought at MTR stations, the airport and tourist information centres. You pay a deposit of HK$50 for the card, then charge it up (minimum HK$150). You swipe the card on special machines each time you board a train, bus, tram, etc, and the fare is deducted; once your initial amount runs out, you can recharge the card at machines at MTR stations, 7–11 and Circle-K convenience stores, as well as supermarkets, which also accept payment by Octopus. For details, see www.octopuscards.com.

Tourist Passes are a more limited option than the Octopus. The **MTR 1-day Tourist Pass** gives you a day's unlimited travel on the MTR for HK$50; the 3-day **Transport Pass** gives you three days' travel on the MTR and some bus routes,

Shopping for fresh produce

including one (HK$220) or two (HK$300) Airport Express trips. Both types of pass are available from Airport Express and MTR stations and tourist information centres.

Getting around: the MTR

The Mass Transit Railway (MTR) is a fast, efficient, clean, air-conditioned rail network that runs daily from around 6am to 12.30/1am. As well as the Airport Express, it has ten lines. Adult single fares range from about HK$4 to HK$26. All stations have automatic machines where you can buy tickets or recharge your Octopus card (see page 130). There are rarely toilets at stations and never on trains, and smoking, eating and drinking are forbidden throughout the MTR.

MTR stations are well signposted in English and Chinese; on the train, each stop is announced in Cantonese, Mandarin and English. Most stations have several exits, identified by letters and numbers, so it's useful to have an idea of which you want; however, there are good local area maps at all stations, and lists of major nearby buildings and roads by all station exits. For more information, tel: 2881 8888 or visit www. mtr.com.hk.

Getting around: buses

Bus routes, run by several companies, cover every part of the SAR, but are most handy for areas not on MTR or rail lines, such as the south side of Hong Kong Island and much of the New Territories. Most run 6am–midnight, but

some operate all night, and night buses run on several other routes.

Most city buses are British-style double-deckers. Drivers rarely speak much English, but each stop has route maps and timetables in English and Chinese. Non-Octopus fares range from a few dollars to HK$45. Note that drivers do not carry change, so if you don't have an Octopus card or a Transport Pass (see page 130), you must have the exact change.

Many routes begin from or run via one of four large termini: at the Central Ferry Piers, beneath Exchange Square and by Admiralty MTR on Hong Kong Island, and the Star Ferry Concourse in Tsim Sha Tsui.

Bus information

You can pick up free **maps** of main bus routes at HKTB Information Centres.
Discovery Bay Transportation Services: tel: 2987 0208; www.hkri.com.
Kowloon Motor Bus (KMB): tel: 2745 4466; www.kmb.com.hk.
New Lantao Bus Company: tel: 2984 9848; www.newlantaobus.com. Serves all of Lantau.
New World First Bus: tel: 2136 8888; www.nwstbus.com.hk. City routes, and many to the New Territories.

Getting around: minibuses

Sixteen-seater minibuses are another option: 'red' minibuses (they are actually cream-coloured, but with a red stripe) run on fixed routes in the city, and 'green'

The MTR is an efficient service

minibuses (cream with a green stripe) run to many small destinations, especially in the New Territories.

Destinations are usually written in English at the front of the van; minibuses stop anywhere, so call out clearly when you want the driver to stop (try *lee do* in Cantonese). Fares vary from a few dollars to HK$20. On red minibuses, you pay as you get out, and drivers do not usually have much change, though on some routes you can use Octopus cards. Exact change or an Octopus card are needed for green minibuses.

Getting around: trams

Trams have rattled all the way along the north side of Hong Kong Island since 1904, and the double-decker carriages are a great-value means of seeing the city. Stops are frequent, and you can hop on and off as you please.

The flat fare is HK$2.30 (HK$1.20, HK$1.10, under-12s, over 65s); exact change is required, or use the Octopus card or a Transport Pass (see page 130). Trams run daily 6am–1am. You get on at the back and get off at the front, paying as you get off. Avoid lunchtimes and rush hours, and head up to the front of the top deck.

The **Peak Tram** is actually a funicular railway, up to the Peak Tower (see page 54).

Hong Kong Tramways: tel: 2548 7102; www.hktramways.com.
Peak Tram: tel: 2522 0922; www.the peak.com.hk.

Getting around: star ferries

These green-and-white, open-sided little ferries run back and forth between the Central Ferry Piers (Piers 7 and 8) and Wan Chai on Hong Kong Island and Tsim Sha Tsui and Hung Hom in Kowloon. They run daily 6.30am–11.30pm, every 6–12 minutes, and the trip takes about eight minutes. Octopus cards are valid. At HK$3.40 (upper deck) and HK$2.10 (lower deck),
Star Ferry Information: tel: 2367 7065; www.starferry.com.hk.

Getting around: taxis

Taxis are abundant and easy to hail on the street, outside rush hours. Taxis come in three colours: red on Hong Kong Island and Kowloon, green in the New Territories and blue on Lantau.

Hong Kong taxis are cheap: minimum fare for red cabs is HK$22, with extra charges for luggage placed in the car boot, booked cabs, and tunnel and bridge tolls. All fares are metered, and receipts given. By law passengers must wear seat belts. To call for a cab, tel: 2571 2929.

Many taxi drivers speak some English, but it's wise to ask someone at your hotel desk to write your destinations down in Chinese; also, all cabs are equipped with radio phones, and somebody at the control centre should be able to translate.

Ferries to the outlying islands

Ferries to Lamma, Lantau and Cheung Chau leave from Piers 3, 4, 5 and 6 of the

Signage is clear

A local bus

Central Ferry Piers, near the Star Ferry Piers in Central on Hong Kong Island. Two types operate on most routes: standard ferries and slightly more expensive fast ferries. Standard ferries are slower but have outdoor decks with great views.

New World First Ferry has the most routes. Fares vary greatly (and may be slightly more at weekends and holidays) but start from around HK$17. Octopus cards can be used on most ferries; otherwise, take the correct money, as change booths are only open at peak times. If visiting Lamma, be aware that there are two routes: one to Yung Shue Wan, the other to Sok Kwu Wan.

Outlying islands ferry information

Discovery Bay Transportation Services: tel: 2987 0208; www.hkri.com. Ferries to the south side of Lantau.

Hong Kong Kowloon Ferry: tel: 2815 6063; www.hkkf.com.hk. To Lamma.

New World First Ferry: tel: 2131 8181; www.nwff.com.hk. Runs to most of the islands.

Ferries to Macau and Mainland China

Turbojet (tel: 2859 3333; www.turbo jet.com.hk) runs ferries 24 hours a day, 365 days of the year to Macau from the Shun Tak Centre's Macau Ferry Terminal, west of the Central Ferry Piers, and China Ferry Terminal in Tsim Sha Tsui, Kowloon. Cotai Jet ferries (www.cotaijet. com.mo) run from the same locations in Hong Kong to the ferry terminal on Taipa.

Turbojet also runs direct ferries to Macau from Hong Kong Airport, and less frequent ferries from China Ferry Terminal to ports in Mainland China, and from the Airport to Shenzhen.

Trains to the New Territories and Mainland China

The MTR network (see page 131) includes four lines serving the New Territories. Trains are fast and frequent: every 3–10 minutes, 5.30am to 12.30–1am daily, and the full trip on East Rail takes 42 minutes, on West Rail 30 minutes. Fares cost under HK$40, and you can use Octopus cards. Many stations are hubs for local bus routes. For MTR Information tel: 2881 8888; www.mtr.com.hk

There are trains roughly once an hour daily, 7.30am–7.15pm, from Hung Hom station in Kowloon to Guangzhou via Shenzhen. If direct tickets to Guangzhou are sold out, take the East Rail line to the border at Lo Wu. The Shenzhen station is a few minutes' walk across the border.

Visas

Most visitors only need a valid passport to enter Hong Kong. British citizens are given six months to stay; nationals of other EU countries, Australia, Canada, New Zealand the US get three months. Your passport must be valid for at least a month beyond your planned date of departure. Visit www.immd.gov.hk for comprehensive information.

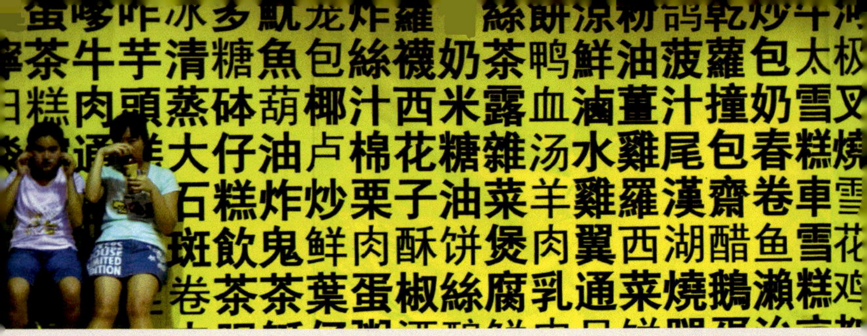

LANGUAGE

Hong Kong's official languages are Chinese and English. The main Chinese dialect is Cantonese, an inseparable part of the sound and rhythm of the city. Mandarin Chinese (Putonghua), the official language of the People's Republic of China, is gaining in popularity, reflecting the importance of doing business with the mainland and of inbound tourism. Cantonese can seem rather daunting to speakers of European languages, but an attempt at a simple phrase or two will generally be well received.

A language minefield

Hong Kong people use a standard form of Cantonese when they write, or in a business situation, but use colloquial Cantonese in everyday conversation. Colloquial Chinese is rich in slang, and some spoken words do not have characters.

Hong Kong (like Taiwan) uses a different style of characters to the rest of China. During reforms initiated by Mao in the 1950s to increase literacy, the People's Republic of China simplified its characters. Hence the characters used on the mainland are referred to as Simplified Chinese, while Hong Kong's more complex characters are called Traditional Chinese.

If all this was not enough to master, there are also Cantonese tones, with each word having a distinct pitch that goes higher, lower or stays flat within each word. Among the Cantonese there is no real agreement as to how many tones there are – some say as many as nine – but most people use six in daily life.

Pronunciation

j as in the 'y' of yap
z similar to the sound of 'ge' in be**ig**e
c as in chip
au as in how
ai as in buy
ou as in no
i as in he

Numbers

0 *ling*
1 *jat*
2 *ji*
3 *saam*
4 *sei*
5 *ng*
6 *luk*
7 *cat*
8 *baat*
9 *gau*
10 *sap*
11 *sap jat*
12 *sap ji*
20 *ji sap*
21 *ji sap jat*
100 *baak*
140 *jat sei ling*

Useful pictorials

Common expressions

Hello *Nei hou (neigh ho)*
Good morning *jo sahn*
Good afternoon *ng on*
Good night *zou tau*
Goodbye *jo geen*
Hello (on phone) *wai!*
Thank you (service) *m goi*
Thank you (gift) *daw jeh*
You're welcome *msai*
No problem *mou man tai*
How are you? *Nei hou maa? (neigh ho marr)*
Fine, thank you *gay ho, yau sum*
yes *haih*
no *mhai*
Please take me to *m goy chey ngor hur-ee*
left *hai jor bin*
right *hai yau bin*
My name is… *ngor geeu*
yesterday *kum yut*
today *gum yut*
tomorrow *ting yut*
hotel *zau dim*
key *so si*
manager *ging lei*
room *haak fong*
telephone *din wa*
toilet *ci so*
bank *ngan hong*
post office *yau jing guk*
passport *wu ziu*
restaurant *zaan teng*
bar *zau ba*
bus *ba si*
taxi *dik si*
train *fo ze*

Questions

Who? *bin go a?*
Where? *bin do a?*
When? *gei si a?*
Why? *dim gaai a?*
How many? *gei do a?*
How much does that cost? *gay daw?*
Do you have…? *yau mo … a?*
What time is the train to Guangzhou…? *Guangzhou ge for che, gay dim hoy a?*

Adjectives

small *sai*
big *daaih*
good *ho*
bad *waaih*
expensive *gwai*
cheap *pehng*
slow *maan*
fast *faai*
pretty/beautiful *leng*
hot *jit*
cold *dung*
very… *hou …*
delicious *ho sick*

Health and emergencies

I have (a) … *ngo…*
headache *tau tung*
stomach ache *tou tung*
toothache *nga tung*
fever *faat sui*
I am sick *ngo jau beng*
doctor *ji sang*
nurse *wu si*
ambulance *gau surng che*
police *ging chaat*

A scene from In the Mood for Love

BOOKS AND FILM

Much has been written and screened about Hong Kong, and numerous literary and cinematic stories told against a Hong Kong backdrop. For a territory of seven million – many with little time for either art form – it is testament to the few that do that literary festivals for both adults (www.festival.org.hk) and children (www.youngreadersfestival.org.hk) are held in March, along with a number of film festivals (see page 20).

The passing of Sir Run Run Shaw, the elder statesman of local film and TV industries, in January 2014, reminded all of Hong Kong's place as entertainment capital of East Asia. He was the pioneer who took kung fu to the west, in the form of Jet Li, though other stars of the genre, such as Bruce Lee and Jackie Chan, also made an impact outside of Shaw Studios.

Oscar-winning **Crouching Tiger, Hidden Dragon** (a joint production between Hong Kong, mainland China, Taiwan and the US) gave international filmgoers an appetite for stylised kung fu period dramas, as did the works of Hong Kong/Hollywood director John Woo. It was several decades earlier, however, that US blockbusters first used the territory as the background for the iconic **Love is a Many Splendored Thing** and **The World of Suzie Wong**.

For a taste of modern Hong Kong movies, watch films by art-house director Wong Kar-wai (**Chungking Express, In the Mood For Love**) or the outrageous Fruit Chan (**Little Cheung, Made in Hong Kong, Durian Durian**).

Books

Non-fiction

East and West by Christopher Patten. The last British Governor's insider account of the handover of Hong Kong to China in 1997.

Gweilo: Memories of a Hong Kong Childhood by Martin Booth. An amusing, affectionate account of an English boy left free to explore the hidden corners of 1950s Hong Kong.

A History of Hong Kong by G.B. Endacott. Long considered the 'Bible' of Hong Kong history, an exhaustive study of the former British colony.

Hong Kong by Jan Morris. Wonderfully insightful text about the economy and people from the doyenne of modern travel writers.

Hong Kong: China's New Colony by Stephen Vines. A thorough overview of the economy, media and political set-up of modern Hong Kong.

Macau: The Imaginary City: Culture and Society, 1577 to Present by Jonathan Porter. The lowdown on this former Portuguese colony.

The Dark Knight featured Hong Kong–set scenes

No City for Slow Men by Jason Ng. The prolific blogger's second volume of essays on the social mores of Hong Kong.

Streets by Jason Wordie. A fascinating guide to the history of individual roads on Hong Kong Island.

Tell Me a Story: Forty Years of Newspapering in Hong Kong and China by Kevin Sinclair. The inside story of how recent Hong Kong history unfolded, from a late great SAR-based journalist.

Fiction

A Girl Like Me and Other Stories by Xi Xi. One of two books of short stories from a leading Hong Kong writer.

The Monkey King by Timothy Mo. A brilliant account of a dysfunctional family living in colonial Hong Kong.

Taipan by James Clavell. A classic about the rise of an influential 19th-century British merchant family in Hong Kong.

A Taste for Intensity by Dominique Perregaux. This account of a Western Hong Kong-based art dealer in Hong Kong and elsewhere offers 21st-century reflections on the city.

The World of Suzie Wong by Richard Mason. A British artist falls in love with a local girl in the book that made Wan Chai famous.

Films

Love is a Many Splendored Thing (1955). This classic Hollywood tear-jerker, set in the early 1950s during the Korean War, depicts the charm and exoticism of colonial Hong Kong, and the problems of inter-racial romance. With William Holden and Jennifer Jones (Hollywood could not then accept a real Chinese actress), the film won three Oscars.

The World of Suzie Wong (1960). A romance between an (changed from the book) American artist (Holden again) and a beautiful local bar girl (the Chinese actress, Nancy Kwan). Filmed extensively on location, most famously in Wan Chai.

Chungking Express (1994). Director Wong Kar-wai creates parallel stories about two lovesick policemen. Tsim Sha Tsui's Chungking Mansions gives the film its English title.

In the Mood for Love (2000). Another Wong Kar-wai production, this tale of unrequited love in the 1950s and 1960s features Hong Kong favourites Maggie Cheung and Tony Leung.

The Dark Knight (2008). Batman hit Hong Kong in style in this Academy Award-winning film. Christian Bale's caped crusader leaps from the IFC Tower during his pursuit of the evil mafia accountant, Lau (a feat previously accomplished by Angelina Jolie's characters in *Lara Croft Tomb Raider: The Cradle of Life*).

Echoes of the Rainbow (2009) Funded by the government's film development fund, it depicts the joys and struggles of life in 1950s Hong Kong.

ABOUT THIS BOOK

This *Explore Guide* has been produced by the editors of Insight Guides, whose books have set the standard for visual travel guides since 1970. With top-quality photography and authoritative recommendations, these guidebooks bring you the very best routes and itineraries in the world's most exciting destinations.

BEST ROUTES

The routes in the book provide something to suit all budgets, tastes and trip lengths. As well as covering the destination's many classic attractions, the itineraries track lesser-known sights, and there are also excursions for those who want to extend their visit outside the city. The routes embrace a range of interests, so whether you are an art fan, a gourmet, a history buff or have kids to entertain, you will find an option to suit.

We recommend reading the whole of a route before setting out. This should help you to familiarise yourself with it and enable you to plan where to stop for refreshments – options are shown in the 'Food and Drink' box at the end of each tour.

For our pick of the tours by theme, consult Recommended Routes for… (see pages 4–5).

INTRODUCTION

The routes are set in context by this introductory section, giving an overview of the destination to set the scene, plus background information on food and drink, shopping and more, while a succinct history timeline highlights the key events over the centuries.

DIRECTORY

Also supporting the routes is a Directory chapter, with a clearly organised A–Z of practical information, our pick of where to stay while you are there and select restaurant listings; these eateries complement the more low-key cafés and restaurants that feature within the routes and are intended to offer a wider choice for evening dining. Also included here are some nightlife listings, plus a handy language guide and our recommendations for books and films about the destination.

ABOUT THE AUTHORS

UK-born print and radio journalist, Andrew Dembina has lived in Hong Kong since 1992. His writing and radio work have focused mostly on lifestyle topics and features for local and international English-language publications, websites and guidebooks on Hong Kong and southern China. He is the author of *Insight Guides Select Hong Kong*. This book is based on original content by Ruth Williams, who has lived in Hong Kong for more than 20 years, contributing to many local and international publications, as well as several *Insight Guides* titles.

CONTACT THE EDITORS

We hope you find this Explore Guide useful, interesting and a pleasure to read. If you have any questions or feedback on the text, pictures or maps, please do let us know. If you have noticed any errors or outdated facts, or have suggestions for places to include on the routes, we would be delighted to hear from you. Please drop us an email at insight@apaguide.co.uk. Thanks!

CREDITS

Explore Hong Kong
Contributors: Andrew Dembina
Commissioning Editor: Sarah Clark
Series Editor: Sarah Clark
Pictures/Art: Tom Smyth/Shahid Mahmood
Map Production: original cartography
Stephen Ramsay, updated by Apa
Cartography Department
Production: Tynan Dean and Rebeka Davies
Photo credits: 123RF 74; Alamy 51R, 84,
136, 137; Alex Havret/Apa Publications
4TL, 4MC, 5MR, 20/21, 32/33, 33R, 35R,
36, 36/37, 38, 39, 43, 48, 80, 81, 83R,
85, 109R, 110, 110/111, 111R, 120,
121, 134; Dreamstime 66, 82, 86; Getty
Images 22/23, 52, 82/83; HKTB 20, 21R,
24MC, 56, 76, 77, 118, 119; Leonardo
96, 97; Mandarin Oriental Group 94MC,
94MR, 100, 100/101, 101R, 103R, 105,
108; Ming Tang-Evans/Apa Publications
1, 2MC, 2MR, 2ML, 2ML, 2MR, 2MC,
2/3T, 4ML, 4BC, 5T, 5M, 5MR, 6ML, 6MR,
6MC, 6ML, 6MC, 6MR, 6/7T, 8, 8/9, 9R,
10, 11, 12, 12/13, 13R, 14, 14/15, 15R,
16, 17, 18, 18/19, 19R, 24ML, 24MC,
24ML, 24MR, 24MR, 24/25T, 26/27, 28,
28/29, 29R, 30, 31, 32, 34, 34/35, 37R,
40, 40/41, 41R, 42, 44, 45, 46, 47, 49,
50, 54, 54/55, 55R, 56/57, 57R, 58, 59,
60, 61, 62/63, 64, 64/65, 65R, 67, 68,
68/69, 69R, 70, 70/71, 71R, 72, 73, 75,
87, 88, 88/89, 89R, 90, 91, 92, 92/93,
93R, 94ML, 94MC, 94ML, 94MR, 94/95T,
106, 107, 108/109, 115, 116, 117T,
117B, 122, 123, 124, 125, 126/127, 128,
129, 130/131, 132, 132/133, 133R, 135;
Peninsula Hotels 112/113; Robert Harding
50/51, 78/79; Shangri-La Hotels 98, 99,
102, 104; SuperStock 53; The Peninsula
102/103, 114
Cover credits: Hong Kong tram by night,
4Corners Images **Front Cover BL:** Boat in
Hong Kong, *Alex Havret/Apa* Publications
Back Cover: (Left) Chinese New Year, *Ming
Tang-Evans/Apa* (**Right**): view from Tsim
Sha Tsui, *Ming Tang-Evans/Apa*

Printed by CTPS – China
© 2014 Apa Publications (UK) Ltd
All Rights Reserved

First Edition 2014

DISTRIBUTION

Worldwide
APA Publications GmbH & Co. Verlag KG
(Singapore branch)
7030 Ang Mo Kio Ave 5, 08-65
Northstar @ AMK, Singapore 569880
Email: apasin@singnet.com.sg
UK and Ireland
Dorling Kindersley Ltd (a Penguin Company)
80 Strand, London, WC2R 0RL, UK
Email: sales@uk.dk.com
US
Ingram Publisher Services
One Ingram Blvd, PO Box 3006, La Vergne,
TN 37086-1986
Email: ips@ingramcontent.com
Australia and New Zealand
Woodslane
10 Apollo St, Warriewood NSW 2102,
Australia
Email: info@woodslane.com.au

INDEX

MAP LEGEND

● Start of tour	★ Place of interest	Park
→ Tour & route direction	ⓘ Tourist information	Important building
❶ Recommended sight	⚊ Statue/monument	Hotel
❷ Recommended restaurant/café	✉ Main post office	Transport hub
	🚌 Main bus station	Souk/market/store
	☾ Mosque	Pedestrian area
	☵ Viewpoint	Urban area